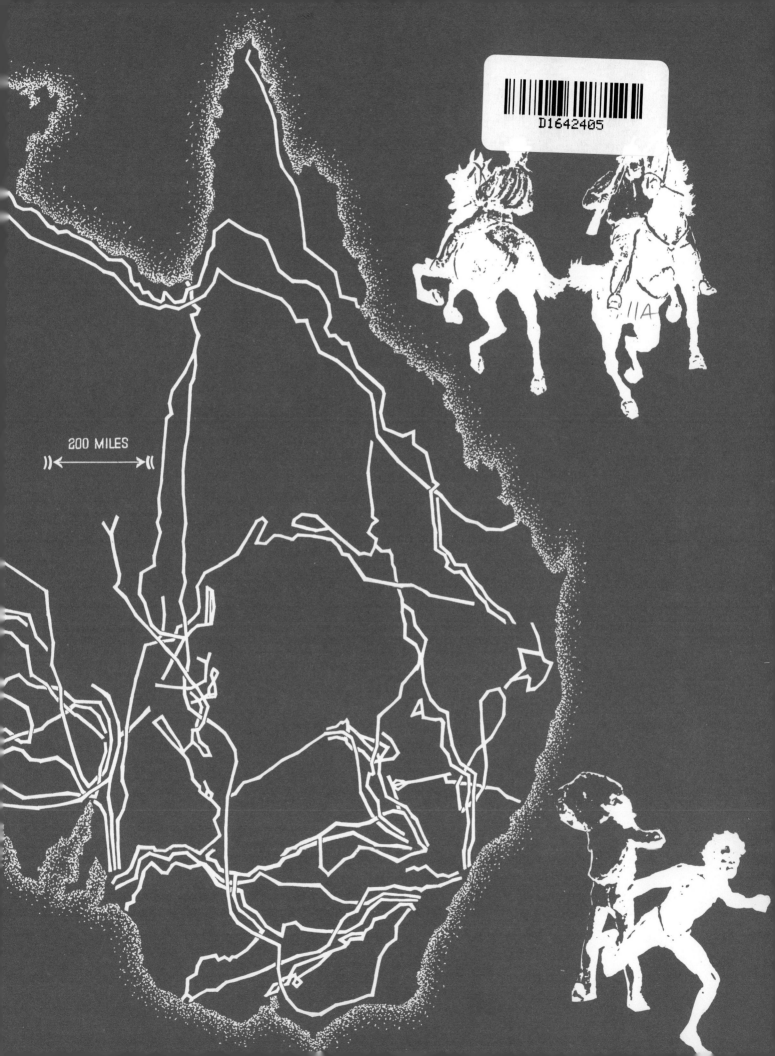

200 MILES

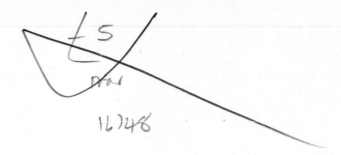

£5

17148

In the steps of the explorers

IN THE STEPS

OF THE EXPLORERS

Jeff Carter .. ANGUS AND ROBERTSON

To Karen, Thor, Goth, and Vandal,
who always wanted to know what their father
was doing out in the bush for so many years

Front cover: Hume and Hovell, *from the*
original in the Mitchell Library, Sydney

The author thanks Dr Jim Hagen, historian at the
Wollongong University College; the many outback
dwellers who put him on the right track at various
times; Mare Carter, for driving, campfire cooking,
note-taking; and the Mitchell Library, where he
read most of the original journals of exploration.

National Library of Australia
registry number Aus 69-3075

SBN 207 95141 1

First published in 1969 by
ANGUS & ROBERTSON LTD
221 George Street, Sydney
107 Elizabeth Street, Melbourne
89/95 Anson Road, Singapore
54 Bartholomew Close, London

© Jeff Carter 1969

Registered in Australia for
transmission by post as a book
PRINTED IN AUSTRALIA
BY HALSTEAD PRESS, SYDNEY

Contents

Here be giants . .

On many ancient maps, when much of the world was unexplored by Europeans, the words "Here be Giants" were inscribed across unknown lands. Only a century ago, when much of inland Australia was unexplored territory, giants did stalk this continent.

They were our early explorers. Men like Sturt, Eyre, Gregory, McKinlay, Stuart, the Forrest brothers, Giles and others. Even the tragic, comic-opera characters of exploration, Ludwig Leichhardt and Robert O'Hara Burke, were big men of a sort—though their foolhardiness brought them and their luckless followers to miserable, dreadful deaths.

Only giants among men could have accomplished the tasks Australia's explorers attempted. No other continent has proved so inhospitable, so dangerous and apparently antagonistic to the prying out of her dry and deadly secrets. In other lands there had been great rivers to follow, fruit, game and fish, reliable pastures and rainfall—and above all, at least a similarity with known lands.

But Australia broke all the rules. What rivers there were in the inland proved fickle strings of waterholes, likely to dry up behind the advancing explorer and cut off his retreat.

The plant life of the arid hinterland was sparse and unsustaining for man or beast in comparison with the lush vegetation of more bounteous lands. On the endless, silent plains of the interior, no herds grazed to provide easy meat for travellers. The only sizeable beast, the improbable, unpalatable kangaroo, was rarely encountered in the far inland and proved difficult to hunt in the open, often treeless, country. Fish and wildfowl were rarely encountered, except on isolated waterholes sometimes a thousand miles apart.

Worst of all in this strange, forbidding country where the trees shed their bark instead of their leaves and rivers dwindled to nothing downstream instead of growing in size, there were no regular, reliable seasons. Europeans accustomed to a cold winter, followed by a thaw, then a lush spring and reliable summer rainfall, took years to learn that Australian seasons were unpredictable, erratic and tremendously prolonged in comparison with European conditions.

This was particularly so inland, where the greatest treks of exploration were attempted. There, on the timeless plains of loneliness, two conditions prevailed—dry and wet. Dry seasons could be years long. Sometimes the wet season came in the cooler "winter" months, sometimes in the hot "summer" period.

Rain, when it did come, was rarely abundant, and the land quickly dried

On the travels of Jeff Carter

What kind of men were the explorers of Australia? What hardships faced them and how well did they overcome their difficulties? Did they attack their self-appointed tasks with skill and commonsense, combining bushcraft and doggedness to achieve their ends—or did they just bungle through?

Were they the best men available for the jobs they undertook? Did they perform well, or indifferently, or badly? Could other men have done the job better?

To find answers for these questions, I have spent much of the past 15 years retracing the routes of the early explorers and reading their original journals. This has involved over 300,000 miles of travel by Land Rover and some 40 original journals and scores of other historical volumes.

I took up the challenge to try to recapture the problems and privations of travel in the 1800s. In this age of radio and aircraft it is rarely possible to experience the sense of isolation the explorers must have known. Fourwheel drive vehicles can in a few days traverse deserts that would have taken horses or camels several weeks. Man-made watering places now provide for the traveller where the early explorers would have perished.

Even so, retracing the journeys of Australia's early explorers can be arduous, even dangerous at times.

up under the blazing centralian sun. Plains briefly green after a shower soon returned to their normal ochre brown or red. Explorers lucky enough encounter good seasons returned to find their Promised Land reduced parched wasteland.

There seemed no pattern to the weather that might aid the planning expeditions.

Even the native inhabitants of this strange, forgotten continent, the aborigines, were regarded as of little use to the explorers. Their way of li appeared so mean and lowly by European standards as to be not worthy attention. They ate lizards, grubs, ants, plant roots, grass seeds and reptile garnering their wretched meals by means that were almost beneath the notic of white men. They were no help to the explorers in finding or supplyin acceptable food. Many of their waterholes turned out to be no more tha depressions scratched in dry sandy creekbeds—of little use to a string of horse or camels, except in emergency.

Some explorers such as Burke and Wills perished in country well popu lated with healthy well-fed aboriginal men, women and children.

Most of the fertile lands had been discovered in the first half century of the colony of New South Wales. By 1839, nearly all of the rich coaste crescent, from Moreton Bay to Adelaide, had been explored. Probably th richest harvest of new lands was made when a practical way was found through the Blue Mountains in 1813 by Blaxland, Wentworth, Lawson an Evans.

Then access to Queensland's lush inland plains was discovered in 1823 b Allan Cunningham, who first found a way through the Liverpool Ranges a Pandora's Pass near what is now the Scone district. In the following year 1824, the squabbling partners Hume and Hovell skirted inland of the Aust ralian Alps and pushed south to Port Phillip Bay. Sturt probed into the middl west of New South Wales in 1828, discovering the Darling River, and wen down the Murray to its mouth in 1830. Major Mitchell traversed westerr Victoria to Portland Bay in 1836. In 1838, gentleman Joseph Hawdor pioneered a stock route from Albury to Adelaide. Cattleman Angus McMillar pushed down from the Monaro plains to discover the rich Gippsland area i 1839.

And so the job was largely done.

The great disappointment for most of the explorers of Australia's inland was that they found nothing worthwhile. No bountiful inland sea awaited Sturt. No rich plains or forests opened before Stuart or Giles. No lush tropical garden, bounteous rivers or great herds rewarded any explorer of the remote inland. Out there was only silence, dry and infinite.

Much of the country today is in worse shape than it was a hundred years ago—with the deterioration of the landscape brought about through over grazing and the introduction of such pests as rabbits and goats. Though the fertile lands are more settled, the deserts are now larger and more forbidding than ever.

John Oxley	**Allan Cunningham**
Hamilton Hume	**William Hovell**
Thomas Mitchell	**Charles Sturt**

The first men to march across the Australian continent found themselves in a strange, flat landscape of gibbers, sand, spinifex and salt bogs. In all the vast inland they did not find a mountain worthy of the name, only decaying, eroded hills and ridges, which were stony, almost devoid of soil or vegetation, and even more inhospitable than the desolate, waterless plains. Horses

knocked up and died beneath their riders, leaving the explorers to struggle home as best they could. Many expeditions failed and some men died. The introduction of camels by Sir Thomas Elder in the 1860s made it possible for explorers to search out the interior for the hoped-for

10

good lands and inland sea they never found. Their greatest finds were deserts and vast areas of arid lands which remain virtually uninhabited a century later. Mining developments have re-awakened interest in remote country scarcely visited since the days of the first explorers

The first twenty-five years

Barrallier and others

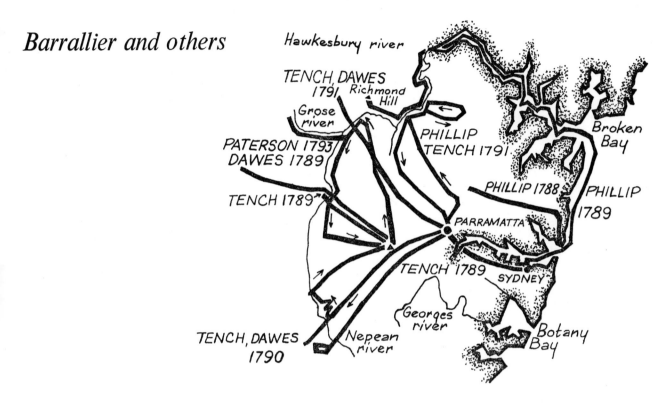

The first Australian explorer was Captain Arthur Phillip. He commanded the First Fleet, which arrived in Port Jackson on 25th January, 1788, after a brief and unsatisfactory sojourn in near-by Botany Bay. In April, Phillip and some of his officers pushed inland for almost 30 miles, as far as what is now Cattai. Next they sailed north to Broken Bay and followed the Hawkesbury River upstream as far as Richmond Hill.

The following year, in 1789, Phillip sent Lieutenant Watkin Tench westward, toward what are now known as the Blue Mountains. Phillip called them the Carmarthen Hills. Tench discovered a large north-flowing stream about 20 miles from the settlement. He called it the Tench. Of this expedition, Phillip reported: "(they) crossed the river, but after the first day's journey they met with such a constant succession of deep ravines, the sides of which were frequently inaccessible, that they returned, not having been able to proceed above 15 miles in 5 days; when they supposed themselves to be 12 miles from the foot of the mountains."

Phillip renamed the stream the Nepean and sent Lieutenants Dawes and Johnston, with surgeon's mate Lowes, to see if they could penetrate the mountains. They reached a high ridge near what is now Linden.

In 1790-1, Tench and Dawes made several more attempts on the mountains, but failed. In 1793, Captain William Paterson led a party into the mountains along the Grose River, but gave up after clambering up five waterfalls in ten miles. In 1794, the former quarter-master of the First Fleet flagship *Sirius*, Henry Hacking, led a party from Parramatta toward the mountains. His notes on the journey are vague, but he claimed to have "penetrated 20 miles farther inland than any other European". He may have followed the Springwood

George Grey   **Edward John Eyre**
Augustus Gregory   **John McDouall Stuart**
Ernest Giles   **John Forrest**

13

Ridge and built the cairn of stones later discovered by Blaxland's party. This cairn was mistakenly attributed to George Caley and misnamed "Caley's Repulse" by Governor Macquarie.

In 1796, Matthew Flinders's shipmate, George Bass tried to climb through the mountains from the Grose River, but failed.

Ex-convict John Wilson, who had spent some time living with the aborigines after serving his sentence, led a walking party south-west from Parramatta in January 1798. The group included a lad called Barracks, some Irish convicts and their guard of soldiers. Governor Hunter had authorized this motley expedition to put an end to the popular convict fiction that there was "a colony of white people at no very great distance in the back country—150 or 200 miles—where there was abundance of every sort of provision without the necessity of so much labour".

Near Picton, the Irish prisoners lost interest and returned to Parramatta with their guards. Wilson, the lad Barracks and a man called Roe continued south to Mittagong, then veered inland, passing Joadja to arrive at the junction of the Wingecarribee and Wollondilly rivers. They returned to Parramatta after being absent for 26 days.

In March, 1798, John Wilson, young Barracks and a man named Collins made a second journey southward of Mittagong through Moss Vale, Bundanoon and Marulan, terminating their journey at Mount Towrang, six miles east of Goulburn. From here they glimpsed the southern end of the Goulburn Plains, 20 miles away.

No one took much notice of Wilson's oral report of his travels (he was illiterate). Notes on the journeys kept by young Barracks, whom Governor Hunter described as "an intelligent lad" were overlooked until 1919. Then a check on their accuracy by a contributor to the *Royal Australian Historical Society Journal* (Volume 4, 1920), indicated that Wilson and his two companions probably were the first Europeans to glimpse the inland plains.

Next man to attempt to get beyond the barrier of the Blue Mountains was Ensign Francis Barrallier, in 1802. He was an adventurous but serious-minded Frenchman who had surveyed and mapped Port Dalrymple and the surrounding country on the Hunter River for Governor King.

Part of Barrallier's map showing his journey to the Abercrombie River

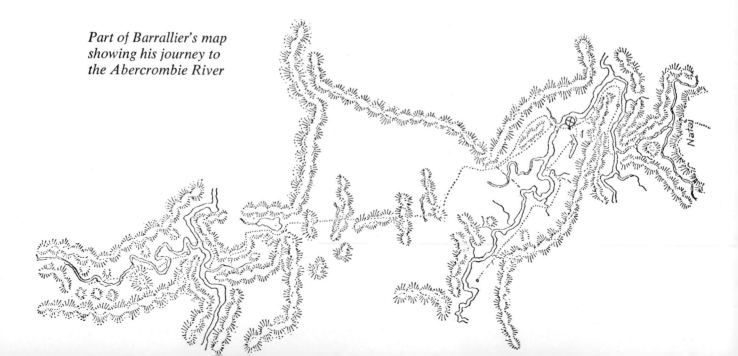

From this it seems he was a conscientious, industrious and competent surveyor, whose maps would be reasonably accurate.

If Barrallier's map of his 1802 journeys is no more than reasonably accurate, then he was undoubtedly the first man to cross the Blue Mountains.

Unfortunately, he has been given credit for getting no farther than Kanangra walls, south of Jenolan Caves. For this to be so, Barrallier's map would have to be utterly wrong—which seems unlikely, in view of the fact that he was regarded by the Governor as a competent surveyor. The map he produced of Port Dalrymple (now Newcastle), has proved accurate enough.

The error concerning Barrallier seems to have arisen because it was assumed that after he crossed the Nepean River near Camden, he began to push westward from what is now Picton. But this is not so. From his map and his journal, it is clear that Barrallier did not head inland until he reached the Mittagong area. This point is only slightly north of Lake Illawarra, and Barrallier's map shows this lake. Most of his journey followed a course almost due west from Lake Illawarra.

His journal clearly states that he travelled about 45 miles slightly west of south from Prospect to his base camp, which brought him close to the present town of Mittagong. Assuming this to be the true starting point of Barrallier's plunge into the mountains, his map checks out well against present-day, highly detailed military survey maps. He apparently went by way of Joadja Hill to the junction of the Wingecarribee and Wollondilly rivers, then westward to the headwaters of the Abercrombie River.

When Barrallier's map of this final section of his journey is compared with his journal, it seems he must have been slightly north of where he supposed himself to be, perhaps by as much as ten miles. He appears to have arrived somewhere on a line between Yalbraith and Porter's Retreat.

In his journal for 22nd November, 1802, he noted that he was now 55 miles from his base camp and 100 from the Nepean River, He pushed on westward another 40 walking miles and on the evening of 25th November, a scout Barrallier had sent to climb a near-by hill reported open country ahead.

That night Barrallier wrote: ". . . everyone . . . congratulated themselves with having succeeded in accomplishing the passage of the Blue Mountains without accident."

Next day, 26th November, Barrallier recorded: "At daybreak, I left with two men to verify by myself the configuration of the ground, and to ascertain whether the passage of the Blue Mountains had really been effected. I climbed the chain of mountains north from us, and when I had reached the middle of this height, the view of a plain as vast as the eye could reach confirmed to me the report of the previous day."

After casting about for a full day trying to find an easy passage down to the plains he could see, Barrallier wrote: "I resolved to follow the stream which dipped to the west." But the going proved rougher than he anticipated. The men, stumbling along the creekbed, their boots falling to pieces and mindful that their rations were almost exhausted, began to complain.

Next day, very reluctantly, Barrallier agreed to turn back. He wrote: "The courage of my men was entirely abated, and nothing but the orders for the return journey would suffice to dispel their melancholy . . . After having cut a cross of St. Andrew on a tree to indicate the terminus of my journey, I returned by the same route I had come."

He was at this point more than 30 miles farther

15

west than Mt York, the terminal point of the Blaxland, Wentworth and Lawson expedition, made 11 years later, in 1813.

Barrallier's expedition had four soldiers, five convicts and a succession of aboriginal guides and helpers. Beyond his base camp near Mittagong, Barrallier took only seven men. He got on exceptionally well with the aborigines, probably because he quite unselfconsciously treated them as fellow human beings—albeit strange ones. He was keenly interested in how they lived, and they responded with friendship and aid.

Barrallier's journal is probably one of the first detailed, authentic studies of how the aborigines lived in their wild state. His observations on everything from their hunting and cooking methods to their intimate family life have proved remarkably accurate. So were his remarks on the plants, birds and animals of the area.

He reported a native "monkey" in the forests, called by the aborigines the "cola", which was probably the koala. Barrallier's chief guides were a man called Gogy and his wife, who travelled with him for much of his journey until they began to worry because they were out of their own tribal territory. Gogy introduced Barrallier to other tribesmen, whom he called "mountaineers", who led the explorer much of the way through the roughest country.

Judging from his meticulous and accurate journal and maps, and from what he accomplished and how he went about it, Ensign Francis Barrallier has a strong claim to the title of the first successful Australian explorer.

For some reason, no one took much notice of Barrallier's exploits—perhaps because his journal was in French and not translated for many years. In any event, his route did not offer easy access to the interior and was therefore of little practical value to the colony.

Botanist George Caley made several direct attempts to cross the Blue Mountains between 1802 and 1806. His best effort was to reach Mt Banks above the Grose River, north of Katoomba. Late in 1806, following Caley's failure, Governor King recorded: "As far as respects the extension of agriculture beyond the first range of mountains, that is an idea that must be given up . . ."

The colony was then in a difficult situation. Army officers and ex-convicts who had been given land grants had proved to be poor farmers. Men like James Ruse, Australia's first successful farmer, were rare. Scarcely sufficient produce was being grown to maintain the colony's increasing population. Drought aggravated the situation.

There was another problem: much good arable land was in the hands of a few powerful men who preferred to use it for grazing. Officers who had amassed considerable wealth from the rum trade had large holdings on which they ran sheep and cattle. John Macarthur had obtained a grant of 5,000 acres in the Camden area, where he built up a large flock of Merino sheep. In 1805, he wrote: "What the demands of Great Britain may be, we certainly may supply it. The universal use of machinery might then be safely sanctioned, and the British Manufacturers would be enabled so to reduce the price of Woollen Cloths, as would secure throughout the world the most complete monopoly that any people ever possessed. We should also participate in the profits of this gainful trade."

Such were the entrepreneurs who formed the nucleus of Australia's landed gentry. The Reverend Samuel Marsden was another who set up a large grazing estate in the early days of the colony.

Wealthy free settlers like the Blaxlands arrived, taking up grants of 8,000 acres for sheep and cattle raising. By the time Governor Macquarie was appointed in 1810, New South Wales was a miniature England, with most of the land held in large estates by a wealthy, powerful, and privileged few.

All the available land, north of the Hawkesbury, south to the Cow Pastures beyond Camden and west to the Blue Mountains was fully taken up, largely for grazing. More land was needed for agriculture. This became a bone of contention between Macquarie and the landed gentry when he tried to make some land available for small farming, particularly by ex-convicts.

The graziers were hungry to expand their empires still further, particularly the sheepmen, who had a rich market in the proliferating spinning mills that came into existence with the English industrial revolution. Several drought years emphasized the need for new pastures.

In 1813, cattle were dying in large numbers. Some of them belonged to Gregory Blaxland, whose large grazing property was located west of Sydney town, near St Mary's, within sight of the mocking Blue Mountains.

Blaxland decided to search out new pastures for his herds, rather than watch them starve. He enlisted the aid of two other landholders, William Charles Wentworth and Lieutenant William Lawson, who was also a surveyor. Being essentially gentlemen graziers, the trio took along on their expedition a convict servant each, plus an experienced bushman, James Burns, five hunting dogs and four pack horses.

For three weeks they slogged westward, hacking a track for the pack horses where necessary and unloading them for the steep descent from Mt York to Cox's River. In this valley they found the pastures they were looking for "sufficient to feed the Stock of the colony . . . for the next thirty years", Blaxland recorded. The party pressed on across the Cox and Lett rivers and ascended Mt Blaxland. From here they could see further good grazing land and decided their mission was accomplished.

". . . provisions being nearly expended . . . clothes and shoes in particular worn out and all . . . ill with Bowel Complaints", the party hastily retraced its steps to Blaxland's property. The journey had taken four weeks.

Blaxland, Wentworth and Lawson had not actually crossed the main dividing ranges to the inland plains and westward flowing rivers. In November of 1813, Governor Macquarie sent out a further expedition to follow up their discoveries.

This was under the leadership of the Assistant Surveyor of the colony, George William Evans. His six-man party included James Burns, who guided the group to the farthest point reached by his previous employers, Blaxland, Wentworth and Lawson.

From here, Evans pushed 98½ miles farther west, to where Bathurst now stands, discovering large tracts of extremely rich grazing land. He encountered emus, kangaroos, ducks and wild geese in abundance. One stream produced so many fine "trout" (Murray cod), he named it the Fish River. This was the second west-flowing stream discovered in the colony. (Barrallier found the first.)

Later, near the turning point of his journey, Evans named the Macquarie River. Here the party feasted on cod weighing up to 15 pounds, and plenty of ducks. "The grass here might be mowed it is so thick and long, particularly on the flat lands," wrote Evans. The flats he named Bathurst Plains.

And so the way to the west was open. The continent was unlocked.

Sydney, Australia's largest city, has spread a mantle of urbanization over most of the country penetrated by our first explorers. The land of Phillip, Tench, Wilson, Wentworth, Blaxland, Lawson and Evans is now patterned by a network of roads, many of them bitumen highways. South to Wollongong, westward to the Blue Mountains and north to the Hawkesbury River, only isolated pockets of land remain untouched by axe, bull-dozer or plough. The rich agricultural and grazing lands straddling the Nepean River are disappearing beneath the suburban sprawl of burgeoning satellite towns. The smoky fingers of industry already touch the mountain ranges that once confined the colony.

Superhighways slash through the Hawkesbury sandstone country; holiday towns dot the Blue Mountains and farther west the smoke of Lithgow's industry drifts inland toward the city of Bathurst. Only the land of Barrallier, bordering the great Warragamba dam, retains much of its pristine beauty and wildness.

The first overlanders

Oxley and Evans

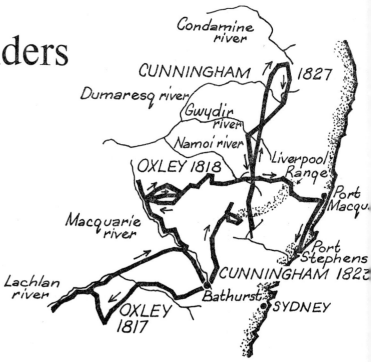

"*The first efficient exploring expedition into the interior of New South Wales was conducted by John Oxley, the Surveyor-General of the colony, in 1817*"—wrote Ernest Giles, in his introduction to *Australia Twice Traversed*, an account of his five expeditions into central Australia.

This is something of a disparagement of George William Evans, whose journeys to Bathurst in 1813 and beyond this to the Lachlan River in 1815 were organized and executed with commendable efficiency. As second in command, Evans accompanied Oxley on his two expeditions in 1817 and 1818.

Oxley's cavalcade was certainly the largest organized exploring party in the history of the colony.

THE JOHN OXLEY EXPEDITION 1817:

John Oxley, in command.
George Evans, second in command.
Allan Cunningham, the King's botanist.
Charles Fraser, the Colonial botanist.
William Parr, mineralogist.
George Hubbard, boat builder.

James King, boatman and sailor.
James King, horse-shoer.
William Meggs, butcher.
Patrick Byrne, guide and horse leader.
William Blake, harness-mender.
George Simpson, surveyor's chainman.
William Warner, servant to Oxley.
Also, 14 horses, rations for five months, guns, fishing lines and kangaroo dogs.

Formed on Governor Macquarie's instructions, the expedition started from Evans's farthest point, on the Lachlan west of Bathurst, and followed the stream inland. For a while, some of the party travelled in two boats built by Hubbard. But the river, fed by storm rains behind them, rose quickly and overflowed its banks to form extensive boggy swamps. The party was forced away from the river and the boats abandoned. This was near Lake Cargellico.

They went south-west into the Hay district, almost to the Murrumbidgee River. Horses and men were perishing through lack of water. The

18

party turned north, regaining the Lachlan in the vicinity of Booligal. Following the river down, they came to low, stagnant lagoons and swamps, near what is now Oxley. This was assumed to be the end of the Lachlan.

Turning back, the explorer noted that the country in which he had been travelling was "uninhabitable, and useless for all the purposes of civilized men". The party followed the Lachlan back to the first swamps, then headed north-east to the Macquarie and traced it home to Bathurst. The journey which began on 28th April, ended on 29th August, 1817.

Nothing of any great interest or value to the colony had been discovered, except that the country deteriorated westward and that one of the two known westward flowing rivers did not end in an inland sea, but petered out in stagnant swamps.

Thus ended "the first efficient exploring expedition into the interior of New South Wales".

Oxley made another journey the following year, in 1818. Setting out again from Bathurst, he followed the Macquarie River north-west.

Once again, Evans was second in command. There were 17 men in the party, 19 horses and two boats.

For a month things went well, some good country being discovered. The deep, clear river offered few obstacles to the boats. Then the land deteriorated, heavy rain fell and the river began to rise.

On the fifth week, the river overflowed its banks 300 miles downstream from Bathurst. Leaving most of his party camped safely on a hill, Oxley sailed another 50 miles downstream, but there lost the course of the river in shallow marshes. He assumed he was on the edge of a huge inland lake or sea, but saw no glimpse of it as his men rowed about fruitlessly among the trees in only a few feet of water.

Oxley rejoined the main party on the hill, where they were marooned for several days after heavy storms. He sent Evans probing the country northeast, toward a distant range of mountains. Oxley stayed with the main body of men at the base camp. Evans returned after ten days, with news that he had crossed another west-flowing stream, which he named the Castlereagh, and had reached the distant mountains.

Rain pelted down for days and Oxley decided to make for the high ground of the ranges beyond the newly discovered river. The country was a continuous, quivering bog in which the horses regularly sank to their girths and had to be unloaded. The men were often struggling waist-deep in water.

The Castlereagh ran a banker and the party had to wait days before they could get across. Hours after they crossed, more rain deluged the country and the river rose ominously, cutting off their retreat. Oxley and his men battled grimly on, unloading the horses when they bogged and manhandling their stores forward to firmer ground. Aborigines watched them, but kept out of the way. Oxley described their "guniahs" (bark huts) in his journal.

Hundreds of kangaroos were seen. One killed was estimated to weigh about 170 pounds. After 17 days, the party reached a small limestone hill five miles west of Mt Exmouth, in what is now the Warrumbungles National Park. This was the point Evans's party had reached earlier. Oxley recorded that his compass behaved in a peculiar fashion on this hill, the needle spinning violently and coming to rest in reverse of the expected position. He named it Loadstone Hill.

East of Mt Exmouth, the party encountered more rain and bogs, but having no alternative, pushed on. With the continuing rain, they had no chance of retracing their outward route to Bathurst. Nineteen days later, they reached the lush plains north of the Liverpool Ranges. Oxley wrote: "We seemed to be once more in the land of plenty." Here were extensive pastures for the colony's sheep and cattle.

The party continued eastward, over country that had recently been flooded. The soil was rich and the vegetation lush. Kangaroos, emus and wild ducks were plentiful. Few aborigines were sighted, but Oxley noted "a great many smokes, arising from the fires of the natives".

In the journals of his two inland journeys, Oxley details many contacts with the aborigines, all of which passed off smoothly. Mostly he surprised young men in trees, while they were searching for possums. Occasionally he came upon a party of women and children. In all cases, the aborigines were initially terrified, but by kindly gestures, Oxley usually managed to get them to accept a tomahawk or some other gift. He observed that in each encounter it was obvious his party were the first white men the aborigines had seen, judging by their fearful consternation.

Once or twice, parties of men shook their spears

in a warlike manner when he was travelling down the Macquarie River, but Oxley ignored them and went on his way. He seemed not to fear a serious attack and never mentions having arms at the ready when approaching aborigines, or setting a guard at night. On one occasion, he invited a group of men into his tents, noting that they were polite, well mannered and careful not to make any action that might give his party offence. Some of them allowed themselves to be shaved.

He found that aboriginal words from the Port Jackson area were not understood among the Lachlan and Macquarie tribes. In fact he recorded no success at all in conversing with them, except in the most trivial manner.

Oxley crossed and named the Peel River near Tamworth, then slogged eastward to the dividing range above Port Macquarie. The descending journey to the coast was a nightmare, through some of the steepest, most treacherous rainforest country in Australia. The horses fell repeatedly and one "literally burst with the violent exertion" and had to be shot. Wind and rain storms plagued the party. Oxley was in constant fear of rockfalls and crashing trees. A monumental descent brought them to the Hastings River, which they followed to the coast, hacking a track through dense jungle.

On the way, Oxley noted the similarity of the brush forest to that of the Illawarra district, mentioning particularly the abundance of red cedar.

At Port Macquarie and farther south at Camden Haven, the explorers saw many aborigines fishing from canoes. Some of the craft were big enough to hold nine men. But the aborigines kept their distance for the most part and were obviously afraid of muskets. Oxley wrote: "They are evidently acquainted with the use of firearms; if any of the people took up a musket, they immediately ran off, and it was only by laying it down that they could be prevailed upon to return, showing by every simple means in their power their dread of its appearance."

Farther south, between Camden Haven and Port Stephens, Oxley's party was several times attacked by aborigines. One man was seriously speared, and on other occasions Oxley and various men had narrow escapes from flying spears. Some of the attackers were men the explorers had earlier treated kindly. In his journal, Oxley expressed his disappointment at their treachery and his determination to have no further contact with them.

It is interesting to note that his troubles began with aborigines who had some previous acquaintance with Europeans—presumably not happy ones, judging from their fear of muskets. Oxley had only friendly contacts with the inland tribes, who had never encountered white men before.

Several wide estuaries barred their way, but with the aid of a boat they found abandoned on a beach, the party eventually struggled south to Port Stephens and Newcastle.

· · · ·

Oxley's westward probing in 1818 resulted in no useful discoveries and brought disappointment to the colony. There were then some 17,500 people in New South Wales, holding between them 225,000 acres of land, of which 93,000 had been cleared. In round figures, 15,000 acres of land had been sown to wheat, 12,000 to maize and a further 2,000 acres to crops such as oats, peas, beans and potatoes. There were in the colony some 3,000 horses, 16,000 pigs, 34,000 cattle and 67,000 sheep.

The industrial revolution was booming at home

"The grave of a native of Australia"—a painting by G. H. Evans to illustrate John Oxley's journals, published in 1820

The junction of the Darling and Murray rivers, where Sturt narrowly dodged a clash with the aborigines. In the foreground, the muddy Darling water, stirred by rain upstream in 1968

National capital, Canberra, stands near the foothills of the Australian Alps, first glimpsed by Major Ovens and Captain Currie, in 1823

The rich Illawarra district, discovered by George Evans in 1812. Then came Dr Throsby, John Oxley, and Hamilton Hume

in England. The new mills were hungry for raw wool. Macarthur and other sheepmen were keen to increase their share of the market. They wanted more land for their flocks. So did the cattlemen, who were being encouraged to go "over the range" to make room for agriculture handy to the settlements at Sydney, Parramatta, Liverpool, Windsor and Newcastle.

Oxley's discovery of the rich Liverpool Plains, beyond the Dividing Range inland from Newcastle, seemed the answer to the colony's problems and aspirations. But how to get there with sheep and cattle? Oxley's devious route, across rivers, marshes and boggy plains, seemed impractical and dangerous. For several years, the Liverpool Plains, so richly described in Oxley's journals, remained an inaccessible Promised Land to the settlers of New South Wales.

By 1822, the need for land, urgent in 1818, became desperate. Botanist Allan Cunningham led several expeditions from Bathurst in attempts to unlock the rich country Oxley had discovered. In 1823, with a small party of five men and five horses, he found and named Pandora's Pass through the ranges between the present towns of Coolah and Quirindi.

Hard on the announcement of his discovery, sheep and cattle were on their way to the newly opened district, which was called the New England district. Three years later, in 1827, Cunningham pushed farther north discovering more rich country, the Darling Downs, inland from the settlement at Moreton Bay. Straying cattle had preceded him most of the way and he recorded his surprise at finding small herds in remote, unsettled areas.

Through the efforts of Oxley and Cunningham, the colony of New South Wales had at last found living space.

The country first seen by Oxley on his journey from Bathurst to the Hay district would be unrecognizable to him now. Huge areas have been cleared for wheat and other cereal crops. Grazing sheep flock on the saltbush plains of the Lachlan and Murrumbidgee country. Great irrigation schemes have transformed much of the land that Oxley would have rejected as unfit for any use into bounteous gardens of plenty.

Dubbo and Tamworth now stand as the capital cities of the wheat and sheep belt through which Oxley and Evans floundered in the rain-drenched year of 1818. Beef cattle range the mountainous country inland from the historic farm and tourist city of Port Macquarie. A rich belt of dairy country runs south to Newcastle, a few miles inland from the coast along which Oxley and his men wearily trudged home.

The New England district, first seen by Cunningham is now highly developed cattle, sheep and orchard country. At Armidale, the nation's first inland university has been established.

South to Hobson's Bay

Hume and Hovell

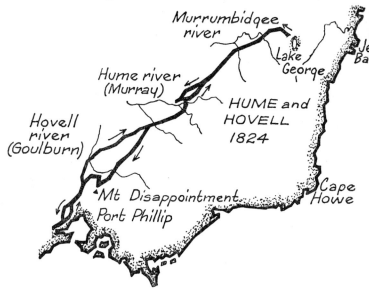

Australia's first native-born explorer of European origin was Hamilton Hume. He was born at Parramatta in 1797. He grew up in this outlying rural area to become a good bushman and friend of the aboriginal tribes in the area. He learned enough of the local dialects to be able to converse with aborigines freely. (He accompanied Capt. Sturt on his first expedition westward to the Darling River and Sturt wrote of him: ". . . I have on all occasions received the most ready and valuable assistance from Mr. Hume. His intimate acquaintance with the manner & customs of the natives . . . chiefly contributed to the peaceable manner in which we have journeyed . . ."

When he was 17, Hamilton Hume, his brother and an aborigine went exploring and discovered good grazing land near Berrima. Charles Throsby, one of the colony's pioneer cattlemen, bought the land to add to his holdings. A few years later, in 1816, surveyor John Oxley was granted land in the Illawarra district and hired Hume to lead his men and cattle to it. In 1817, Governor Macquarie sent Hume with surveyor James Meehan and Throsby to examine the Shoalhaven area and the upper reaches of the river. They returned by an inland route, discovering Lake George and Lake Bathurst on the way. In 1821, Hume discovered Yass Plains and took up land there. In 1822, Hume and Shoalhaven pioneer Alexander Berry journeyed up the Clyde River to what is now Braidwood.

Hume was then established on his property at Yass, where he grazed sheep and cattle. But exploring was in his blood. Some 18 months after his Braidwood trip, he was hankering to set out again into new lands.

Hume was now regarded as one of the finest bushmen in the colony and a reliable trail-blazer to new and useful country. Governor Brisbane approached Hume and asked him to lead a convict exploration party which he planned to put ashore in or near Port Phillip Bay. The idea was that the party would attempt to find a route overland to Sydney.

Hume didn't like the idea, but offered to lead a party from his Yass property to Port Phillip Bay. Governor Brisbane agreed to finance and equip the expedition. Months of protracted negotiations dragged by with little result and the proposed adventure seemed destined never to begin. Then a former ship's captain turned settler, William Hovell, offered to equip the expedition, provided he could join the party. Grasping at straws, Hume agreed. Eventually the Government supplied six pack saddles, some clothing and blankets for the six convicts in the party, six muskets with ammunition and a tent and tarpaulin. Hume and Hovell between them mustered the rest of their requirements, including four bullocks, two carts and three horses, plus flour, salt pork, sugar and other stores.

On 17th October, 1824, the party left Hume's property near Yass.

Rivers and rough country made their carts superfluous. At the Murrumbidgee, a tarpaulin was wrapped round one cart to turn it into a boat for ferrying supplies across the river. More rugged country caused the party to abandon the carts.

Some camp gear had to be left behind, also. The remaining stores were loaded on pack saddles on the four bullocks.

Heading south-west, the party journeyed through the Tumut-Batlow area and were the second Europeans to glimpse the Australian Alps. (Major Ovens and Captain Currie had seen them a year earlier, on their expedition to the Monaro district in 1823.)

The Murray River (which they named the Hume), temporarily halted the explorers. Eventually they crossed it just above its junction with the Mitta Mitta. Tarpaulins were used to "puddingcloth" equipment across the water, a trick Hume said he had learned from Oxley. Discovery of this great west-flowing stream quickened the interest of colonists in the unknown destination of the inland rivers. Hume and Hovell's reports of good grazing land and rich forests dispelled the pessimism generated seven years earlier by Oxley's report from the Hay area: "We have demonstrated beyond a doubt, that no river could fall into the sea between Cape Otway and Spencer's Gulf . . . and that the country south of the parallel of 34 degrees and west of the meridian 147.30 E. was uninhabitable, and useless for all the purposes of civilized men." (That is, south of Hay and west of Albury.)

Soon after crossing the Murray, Hume and Hovell were confronted with more rivers, including the Ovens and Goulburn.

Farther on, they found themselves in conflict with the dividing ranges and veered slightly westward. The country was rough and impenetrable in places, but they eventually made their way through to Port Phillip, by a pass near the present town of Kilmore. They reached the western shores of the bay on 16th December, 1824, but thought they were at Western Port. The journey had taken two months.

Aborigines they met near the beach indicated by miming that a ship had recently been in the bay, farther westward. The party ventured round the shoreline as far as what is now Geelong, where some men thought they heard the distant sound of a ship's cannon.

After some argument, the expedition began the return journey to New South Wales. By taking a slightly more westerly course, they kept clear of the mountains and regained Hume's farm in only one month, half the time of their outward journey.

On their outward journey, the travellers met considerable hardship in crossing rivers, steep country and dense bush, but their greatest trials and tribulations stemmed from personality differences. Throughout the entire expedition, the ill-matched leaders had bickered and argued almost every step of the way. Each time a choice of method or direction had arisen, Hume the bushman had wanted to do one thing, while Hovell the sailor had wanted to do another.

The men had generally sided with Hume. This was no doubt largely due to the fact that Hume, the bushman, was a safer bet than Hovell, the sailor. Hume fraternized with the convicts, whereas Hovell held himself aloof, as his writings in the subsequent controversy confirm. Hovell, the English-born naval disciplinarian, was much more a man of his time than Hume, the native-born, free-wheeling bushman.

The public knew little of Hume and Hovell's bickerings until the city of Geelong decided to celebrate its 30th anniversary in 1854. Hovell was invited by the city fathers and it seems to have been left to him to invite Hume or not, according to his discretion. He chose not to and later defended his decision by claiming that Hume had become "less than a gentleman" with the passage of years and would have been a source of embarrassment to Geelong society.

Newspaper publicity of the celebrations featured Hovell and scarcely mentioned Hume, who immediately set to work writing a pamphlet about the 1824 expedition in which he systematically demolished his erstwhile travelling companion, William Hovell. Hume, thoroughly aroused, went to considerable trouble locating the convicts who had been on the expedition. He found three (two had been his own servants and one had been the servant of Hovell). All three made lengthy written statements in which they criticized Hovell and backed up the story told in Hume's pamphlet. The publication was edited by the Reverend William Ross of Goulburn, who interviewed the three ex-convicts and satisfied himself that Hume's story was justified.

The three men were Thomas Boyd (Hovell's servant), Henry Angel and James Fitzpatrick (Hume's servants).

The gist of Hume's pamphlet entitled *A Brief Statement of Fact* was that Hovell had been a completely worthless member of the expedition. Far from playing a leading role in it, he had been a constant hindrance from the day they encountered their first obstacle, the Murrumbidgee River, when he had wanted to turn back. He had wanted to turn back at every subsequent river and mountain range. He had been useless in the bush, as a worker or innovator, and became lost every time he rode out of sight of the main party (once overnight).

He had split the party several times, turning back with one or more of his servants, but invariably changed his mind and came trailing after Hume when it became obvious the bushman was determined to press on. When the alps had barred their way, he had wanted to veer east and march headlong into them, whereas Hume's bushman's sense told him to veer west and skirt them. When they were confronted with the broad Murray River, Hovell had wanted to go downstream, which would have decreased their chances of crossing as the stream grew broader. To a bushman like Hume it was obvious they would have to go upstream to the narrower headwaters to make a crossing. Hovell had not made astronomical observations to fix and chart their course accurately, as he was supposed to do. He had not done his share of the work, but had left everything to his and Hume's servants, in the manner of a gentleman of leisure.

Boyd, Angel and Fitzpatrick agreed with everything Hume wrote. They also made some interesting observations of their own:

"None of the men had any confidence in Mr. Hovell . . . The long and the short of the story is, I never saw Captain Hovell doing anything in the way of leading or directing . . . all he did was travel on with the men, mostly in the rear of them" —Henry Angel.

"Mr Hume always kept the reckoning of our course and day's progress; it was his regular afternoon's work. I never saw Mr. Hovell do this"— Thomas Boyd. Speaking of the time he was lost overnight with Hovell, Boyd wrote that he decided he would not go out another night with Hovell alone. "That was his first and last expedition by himself," Boyd recorded.

When the party was nearing Hobson's Bay (Port Phillip), Hume remarked that he could see the sea ahead, but Hovell disagreed, saying it looked more like burning grass. Hume then picked up some sea shells from the remains of a native campfire. "Mr Hume pointed to these and asked where they came from. Mr. Hovell replied, from the sea, of course. We made the sea that day . . . Mr. Hovell wished to turn back when we first made the sea and Mr. Hume had much ado to get him on a few miles further . . . Mr. Hovell refused to go on further with Mr. Hume. Mr. Hume, however, went on, and Mr. Hovell called out after him and followed, just as he was getting out of sight. Indeed, he never would have seen the present site of Geelong, but for being obliged to follow Mr. Hume" —Thomas Boyd.

In his pamphlet, Hume claimed that on the day they left Port Phillip, he made a bet with Hovell that they would be back on his property in a month—and they were, to the day. Boyd and Fitzpatrick verified this story.

"As we returned, Mr. Hume would tell us of a morning, that we would cross our outward track that day, and he was always right; we always did; we made a much shorter road home again"— James Fitzpatrick. (The outward journey, measured on "Claude's wheelbarrow"—the perambulator operated by convict servant Claude Bossawa —was 670 miles; the return journey, 520 miles.)

After Hume's pamphlet appeared, Hovell published a reply, but it was singularly brief and unconvincing. His main theme was that Hume's story was backed up only by the statements of ex-con victs, whose words, of course, could not be believed in any circumstances, particularly when they conflicted with those of a gentleman. He made much of the fact that Hume had actually mixed with the men while he, Hovell, had very correctly held himself aloof. He also hinted that Hume retained some form of mysterious influence over the three ex-convicts which enabled him to force them to agree with his claims, even though 30 years had elapsed. Friendship, perhaps.

Summing up, Hume the bushman's story, backed up by his previous record and the written testimony of three others, has the ring of truth about it. Hovell's reply does not. As a final word on the controversy, a historian of the period, Ernest Favenc, recorded that in 1883, Thomas Boyd was the only surviving member of the Hume and Hovell expedition and that he had reiterated that Hamilton Hume deserved the full credit for getting the party through.

Hovell's only memorable achievement, it seems, was to make an error in his astronomical observations and record that the party had reached Western Port instead of Port Phillip Bay. (He set the matter right in 1826, when he visited the Bay in a ship.)

In his journal (apparently written some time after the completion of the 1824 journey) he made a number of sensible observations concerning overland expeditions. These included the suggestion that a tradesman to shoe the expedition horses should be sent with the party, also a saddler and shoe-maker. Somewhat unexpectedly, he seems to have admired the aborigines, pointing out that they were "not the poor wretches as supposed". They had "no house rents or taxes to pay . . . no work except to find food" and ". . . above all, they have their free liberty".

Along the way to Melbourne, Hovell planted clover seed and peach stones—perhaps while Hume and his convict mates were mending the saddles.

Australia's busiest interstate highway now follows the approximate route followed by Hume and Hovell. Thriving sheep and cattle properties straddle the Hume highway from the outskirts of Sydney through Goulburn, Yass, Gundagai, Albury, Wangaratta, Benalla and Seymour to the northern suburban limits of Melbourne. In what is now the Australian Capital Territory, pine plantations cover the slopes beyond which the explorers caught their first glimpses of the Australian Alps. The rugged country of the Batlow area that forced the explorers inland is now dotted with orchards, pine plantations and cleared grazing lands.

The waters of the great Hume dam flood the country where Hume and Hovell passed into Victoria. In the Ovens valley, hops and tobacco crops thrive. Westward of the explorers' route, is the famous Rutherglen wine producing district. The industrialization of cities like Wangaratta foreshadows the imminent urbanization of much of Hume and Hovell's country southward to Melbourne. Geelong, first glimpsed by the explorers, is the State's second largest industrial centre.

Towards the sunset

Sturt

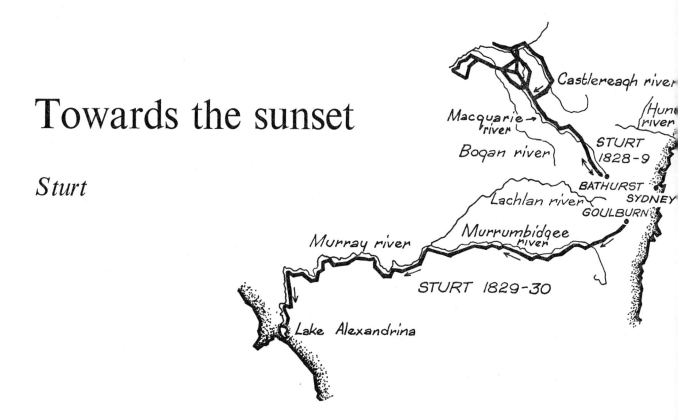

Drought, that great spur to exploration in the early days of settlement, plagued the colony in 1827-8. A year earlier, in 1826, Governor Darling had proclaimed the "limits of location" of the colony, a rough crescent of land extending from the Manning River in the north to the Moruya River in the south and inland to the Bathurst Plains. Settlers were required not to stray beyond this imaginary line which marked the theoretical boundary of the colony. They did, of course, squatting with their sheep and cattle on any good grazing land they could find. This was illegal, but had the advantage of being cheap; Governor Darling had also stated that the land was not available for purchase or lease.

But the spectre of drought spurred Darling to encourage exploration of the mysterious western lands beyond the limits of location. Perhaps somewhere over the horizon were lush green plains to feed the colony's starving stock. The swamps on the Lachlan and Macquarie rivers that had stopped Oxley in 1817 might now be dry enough to cross.

It seemed a good opportunity to solve the mystery of those westward flowing rivers, and might at the same time bring some relief to the settlers' hungry sheep and cattle.

The man Governor Darling chose to probe westward into the forbidding country that had stopped Oxley was his military secretary, Captain Charles Sturt, aged 33. As Sturt's second in command, he appointed Australian-born bushman explorer, Hamilton Hume, aged 31.

The party set out in December, 1828, at the height of one of the hottest, driest summers on record. In addition to the two leaders, there were two soldiers, one free settler and seven convicts in the party. Stores and equipment were carried on a string of packhorses and oxen and several drays, one of which carried a boat.

The Macquarie was a mere trickle compared with the flooded torrent of Oxley's time. After a brief trial, the idea of travelling by boat was abandoned. The once boggy marshes were now a tangle of dry reeds and isolated stagnant pools. Sturt floundered in a labyrinth of dry and drying channels and eventually veered south-west away from the river. He and his men came to the Bogan River on 1st January, 1829. They plodded downstream for a month, observing the plight of drought-stricken aborigines, animals and birds as they went. They discovered the Darling River, which they recognized as a major stream, though it was scarcely flowing and too salty to drink. Sturt

28

followed the Darling downstream for 70 miles, then began his return journey.

On the way back, he traced the Bogan for some distance, then branched overland to meet the Castlereagh, which he followed homeward.

Sturt had solved the mystery of the destination of three inland rivers, the Castlereagh, the Macquarie and the Bogan—they flowed into the Darling. But now there was a greater mystery: what happened to the waters of the Darling?

The west-flowing Murrumbidgee was another mystery. Did it join the Darling, and if so, where did the combined waters end? Governor Darling, no doubt flattered at having a major river named after him, sent Captain Sturt to find out.

The expedition set out on 3rd November, 1829. Sturt's second in command this time was George Macleay, aged 20. Also in the party were three soldiers and a number of convicts. The chief item of equipment was a 27-foot whale-boat, carried in sections on drays.

Meeting the Murrumbidgee near the present town of Jugiong, Sturt and his men tramped down its banks until marshy country threatened to stop them. This was at a point 15 miles upstream from the Murrumbidgee's junction with the Lachlan. A maze of billabongs and boggy channels prevented any further marching, but the main stream was deep enough for boat travel.

Leaving some of his men at a depot camp, Sturt proceeded downstream in the whaleboat with seven companions. It was 7th January, 1830. Two months had passed since the expedition left Sydney town.

Within hours, Sturt passed the junction with the Lachlan, but the river continued narrow and difficult to negotiate. Fallen logs had to be cleared frequently. The river showed every prospect of dwindling to nothing, as the Macquarie and Lachlan had done when Oxley followed them 12 years earlier.

Sturt sailed on for a week, averaging only ten miles or so each day. Aborigines hung about the camps at night, but contact was generally brief and unrewarding—to Sturt at least, who discovered that his supplies and equipment were occasionally pilfered. Relationships continued guardedly friendly, despite these misdemeanours.

On the eighth day of the voyage, the whale-boat abruptly left behind the close banks of the Murrumbidgee and glided out into a much larger, smoothly flowing west-bound stream. Sturt was delighted. This was by far the largest river yet discovered in the colony. He named it the Murray, not realizing it was the stream called the Hume by Hume and Hovell when they crossed it several hundred miles to the east in 1824.

The expedition continued downstream in jubilant mood, their task made easy by the steady current and few obstacles. Shallow water over sandbars was the biggest danger, apart from occasional log snags and isolated rocks. Aided by the current, the whale-boat travelled about 30 miles daily.

The river surface was often low down between steep banks, concealing any view of the surrounding countryside. The travellers saw little but gnarled rivergums looming against blue skies. Aborigines were present in considerable numbers, but contacts remained brief and cautious. Sturt handed out tomahawks and other items to some tribal spokesmen.

Farther downstream, the tribes seemed more warlike. They showed their resentment at the intrusion of strangers by painting themselves and making threatening motions with spears and throwing sticks from the top of the river banks. At the junction with the Darling River, near the present town of Wentworth, a battle seemed inevitable. A large number of armed men assembled on a sand-spit and made it obvious they were prepared to fight rather than let the whale-boat pass.

Sturt and his men were on the point of opening fire when an aborigine they had befriended at an earlier camp suddenly appeared and harangued the warlike mob into lowering their spears.

Sturt had scarcely time to thank his lucky stars for this escape when he observed the Darling River joining the stream on which he was voyaging. After rowing up the Darling a short distance, Sturt deduced that it was the same river he had discovered and named a year earlier, in the vicinity of the present town of Bourke.

So far as Sturt was concerned, another mystery was solved: the Castlereagh, the Macquarie, the Bogan and the Darling all flowed into the Murray, as did the Lachlan and the Murrumbidgee. Where did the mighty Murray end? He sailed on to find out.

Thirty days and 1,000 miles after beginning his voyage, Sturt had found the answer. But the culmination of his journey was disappointing. The Murray did not flow directly into the sea, where a port and city might have been established. Instead, it entered a vast, shallow tidal lake, which in turn gave access to the sea over sand-bars and treacherous narrow channels unsuitable for craft of any size. Sturt named the lake Alexandrina. Lines of breakers prevented access to the sea for the whale-boat. Barren sand dunes devoid of fresh water made a lengthy camp impossible. Sturt had to give up his plan of waiting to sight a passing ship in Encounter Bay, situated beyond the almost land-locked waters of the lake.

There was nothing else for it but to row back the 1,000 miles to his depot camp on the Murrum-bidgee, above the junction with the Lachlan! That nightmare journey ranks high among the epics of endurance in Australian exploration.

On short rations to begin with, starving near journey's end, the weary men rowed homeward against the current from dawn until 7 p.m. each day for 23 days. This brought them to the junction with the Murrumbidgee. Spurred on by the threat of starvation, they accomplished this section of their return journey in three days less time than it had taken them on the outward voyage. Another day brought them to their old depot camp, which they found deserted.

Rain had swollen the river and Sturt decided to proceed upstream as far as possible in the whale-boat. For another fortnight the weary, emaciated men rowed mechanically, gaining less than five miles each day. One man became delirious. Sturt's eyes were badly inflamed and infected. A few para-keets and a swan were added to the dwindling provisions. It was now mid-March, 1830.

Near Hamilton Plains they could go no farther in the boat. Sturt set up camp with five of his companions, sending the two fittest men to the nearest station, some 80 miles away, to get help. Luckily they encountered a relief party and guided it to Sturt's camp.

Months later, the explorer and his men limped into Sydney. Sturt became blind for several months but eventually recovered both his health and his determination to solve the riddle of the inland.

The Bourke district on the Darling River, first penetrated by Sturt in 1829, is today even less hospitable than it was in the explorer's time. Constant grazing and clearing have greatly depreciated the landscape. Wind erosion has left increasing areas of claypan and stony country. The Western Division of the State, where once 12 million sheep grazed, can now support only half that number. The situation is gradually worsening; regeneration of the native vegetation is almost impossible because of constant eating down of young plants by sheep, cattle, rabbits and other introduced animals.

Along the route of Sturt's river voyage to South Australia, the situation is much the same. The Murrumbidgee country downstream from Leeton and Griffith has deteriorated, but conversely the irrigation areas between Mildura and Renmark have made bloom the "desert interior" that so depressed Sturt. The era of the Murray River paddle steamers has passed, but today a few of these historic vessels survive, conveying tourists comfortably over the route that provided so much hardship and privation for its explorers.

Blaxland, Wentworth and Lawson, with three servants and bushman James Burns, crossed the
Blue Mountains in 1813

Overleaf: The Murrumbidgee today is much as it was when Sturt sailed down it and the Murray for 1,000 miles

Charles Sturt confronted by hostile aborigines on his epic voyage down the Murray River in 1830

Hume and Hovell country today. The Goodradigbee on the explorers' route near the town of Wee Jasper

Victoria's west coast was reached by an overland route for the first time by Major Thomas Mitchell in 1836

The jealous major

Mitchell

Although his discovery of the Darling and voyage down the Murray ranked as the most spectacular feats of exploration, Sturt himself was disappointed with his discoveries. He had hoped to locate rich and useful pastures, perhaps surrounding an inland sea, but instead his journeys had taken him into dry, inhospitable, apparently useless country.

He spoke of the Murray as cleaving "a channel through the desert interior" and likened the country downstream from Mildura to the Nile valley of Egypt. Commenting on the seasonal flooding of the lower Murray plains, Sturt wrote: "The natives look to this periodical overflow of their river, with as much anxiety as did ever or now do the Egyptians, to the overflowing of the Nile. To both they are the bountiful dispensation of a beneficent Creator, for as the sacred stream rewards the husbandman with a double harvest, so does the Murray replenish the exhausted reservoirs of the poor children of the desert, with numberless fish, and resuscitates myriads of crayfish that had lain dormant underground; without which supply of food, and the flocks of wild fowl that at the same time cover the creeks and lagoons, it is more than probable, the first navigators of the Murray (Sturt and

party) would not have heard human voice along its banks . . ."

Sturt was not the only man dissatisfied with the fruits of his journeyings. So was the colony's exploring surveyor general, Major Thomas Livingstone Mitchell, but for different reasons.

Mitchell was envious of the reputation that Sturt, a mere captain, had established. A military minded veteran of the Duke of Wellington's campaigns, he believed in large, heavily armed exploring parties and relied more on fire-power than negotiation in his dealings with the "natives". His expeditions were running skirmishes with the aborigines rather than journeys of exploration.

His first effort, in 1831, was inspired by the unlikely story expounded by a recaptured convict who had lived with the aborigines north-west of Sydney for some time. This man told of a great north-westward flowing river and fertile country in the area crossed by Oxley in 1818 and Cunningham in 1827. Neither of these explorers had reported such a river but Mitchell apparently chose to investigate.

Setting out in the favoured starting month of December, 1831, he followed Cunningham's tracks through Pandora's Pass and then followed the Namoi River (discovered by Oxley) downstream for some distance. Then he veered north to the Gwydir (discovered by Cunningham) and followed it downstream to its junction with the Barwon (the lower McIntyre, discovered by Cunningham).

Having failed to penetrate as far west as Oxley or as far north as Cunningham, Mitchell returned to Sydney. All the streams he had crossed were tributaries of Sturt's Darling. This was a bitter pill to swallow.

His mission had accomplished little, apart from proving his convict informant a liar. Mitchell did however record one first: he was the first inland explorer to clash violently with the aborigines, losing two of his men in the process.

Mitchell's second expedition was inspired by his wish to prove wrong Sturt's theory that the Darling River flowed into the Murray. His plan was to follow Sturt's tracks to and down the Darling and then continue on to the river's destination, which he hoped would be the fabled inland sea.

Mitchell set out ahead of the largest expedition yet mounted by the colony. He had 21 men, all heavily armed, seven pack horses, seven bullock carts, two boats and a flock of sheep.

Apart from the usual stores and the novel mutton-on-the-hoof, Mitchell brought along dogs to hunt down kangaroos and emus.

The party set out in March 1835, to follow the Bogan River toward the Darling. But disaster struck only 100 miles beyond Bathurst, just as the party reached the Bogan. The botanist with the expedition, Richard Cunningham (brother of explorer Allan Cunningham), wandered away and got lost. Mitchell camped for three days waiting for him to return, then spent another 12 days searching the area. Cunningham's horse was found dead from thirst. Various items of the botanist's equipment and clothing were picked up. The lost man's tracks were cut several times, but he was never sighted.

Mitchell pressed on to the Darling, where he built a stockade in good military fashion, which he called Fort Bourke. He intended to leave his carts and some of his party here and continue downstream by boat. After building his fort, Mitchell examined the river and found too many sand-bars and snags for boat travel. So he proceeded downstream with his entire party, abandoning his stockade to the curious aborigines, who

may have wondered why Mitchell didn't examine the river *before* building his fort.

Passing the farthest point reached by Sturt (70 miles downstream from Bourke), Mitchell continued on for another 200 miles.

The local tribes showed their resentment at this invasion of their land by firing the grass around the explorers and pilfering stores at night.

Soon the fatal skirmishing that was typical of all Mitchell's expeditions broke out. In one clash, three aborigines were shot down, including an old man and a woman carrying a child.

Following this incident there was open warfare between the explorers and the aborigines. Mitchell, harking back to his military days, at one stage ordered a musket charge at some jeering tribesmen loitering on the outskirts of his camp.

Somewhere near what is now Menindie, the expedition turned back. The men were weary from their 900 mile trek and fearful of a concerted attack from the aborigines. The camp was in a constant state of alert and nervous tension. Several men were ill with scurvy and dysentery.

The party struggled back to civilization, learning at Bathurst that a policeman, W. Zouch, had discovered and buried the remains of Cunningham. The botanist had been killed and partially eaten by aborigines.

Mitchell returned a second time to Sydney with little that was new to report, save further deaths of black and white men. The fact that his only discoveries tended to support Sturt's theory about the Darling must have been salt in his wounds.

A year later, in March, 1836, he was off again with an even larger party, determined to prove Sturt wrong. Mitchell claimed that the river Sturt said was the Darling entering the Murray was in reality the Lachlan. He aimed to prove this by following the Lachlan downstream to the Murray.

He did this, and to his consternation found that the Lachlan joined the Murrumbidgee, which in turn joined the Murray, just as Sturt had recorded. Mitchell then followed the Murray to its junction with the Darling. On the way, the usual skirmishing with local tribes broke out. News came to Mitchell from an aboriginal guide that the Menindie tribe he had fought a year earlier were on their way to extract vengeance.

When the opposing armies met, things were peaceful enough. There was a parley and Mitchell stated that he "endeavoured to establish amicable

36

intercourse between them". How, he does not say, but goes on to complain that one of the aborigines kept examining his cap "as if to ascertain if it was proof against a club"! Mitchell wrote: "The whole tribe watched my motions so attentively that I retired to my tent, leaving the negotiations to Piper" (the aboriginal guide).

These negotiations apparently broke down and the tribes resorted to the common practice of hanging round the camp in a belligerent and annoying manner, catcalling and spear rattling from a safe distance. Many explorers were subjected to this treatment but managed to avoid head-on armed clashes.

Mitchell the military tactician, who had little time for diplomacy, decided to ambush the irritating tribesmen and wipe them out. "Our own safety and further progress evidently depended on our attacking them forthwith," he stated. "It was difficult to come at such enemies hovering in our rear with the lynx-eyed vigilance of savages. I succeeded, however, by sending back a party of volunteers through a scrub to take them in the flank, while I halted the rest of the party suddenly beyond a hill to which the savages were likely to follow us. Attacked simultaneously by both parties, the whole betook themselves to the river, my men pursuing them and shooting as many as they could. Numbers were shot in swimming across the Murray and some even after they had reached the opposite shore . . . In a very short time, the usual silence of the desert prevailed on the banks of the Murray and we pursued our journey unmolested."

Confronted by a large river entering the Murray and his own maps of the Darling between Fort Bourke and Menindie, Mitchell at last accepted Sturt's claim that the Darling flowed into the Murray. He travelled only eight miles up the Darling before conceding that further exploration in that direction was unnecessary.

Once again, Mitchell had discovered nothing new and had little to report except fighting between his party and the aborigines. Determined to make some useful discovery, he pushed south. This time the major's luck changed. He came upon large tracts of rich country with several small but swift-flowing rivers, heading north to join the Murray.

Delighted, Mitchell named the area Australia Felix and skirted west of a range of mountains he called the Grampians. Here he discovered a south-

flowing stream, on which he launched his two boats. The stream, which Mitchell named the Glenelg, carried the explorers to the sea at Discovery Bay, close to the present South Australian border.

Then Mitchell headed overland to Portland Bay, where he was astonished to find the well-established farms of the illegal settlers, the Henty family, from Tasmania. It was now August, 1836. The party had been travelling for six months and supplies were dwindling.

Plotting an almost direct course for Sydney from Portland Bay, Mitchell and his party hurried homeward. On 30th September, on a high point he called Mt Macedon, Mitchell looked south-east toward Port Phillip, 40 miles away. Visibility was clear and he wrote: "I saw a mass of white objects which might have been tents or vessels." He was looking at the settlement on the Yarra River, founded by John Batman and John Pascoe Fawkner, and later to become known as Melbourne.

Beyond Mt Macedon, the explorers were soon in Hume and Hovell country and managed a safe return without further incident. They reached Sydney in November, 1836.

At first Mitchell's discoveries of lush new country were hailed with delight and he was feted throughout the colony. Then the story of his battles with the aborigines became public knowledge and he was loudly condemned by newspapers and leading citizens.

An official enquiry was held, which rebuked the major severely for his treatment of the aborigines. No official action was taken against him, but the judgement deplored his ambush massacre on the banks of the Murray.

Mitchell led a further expedition into Queensland in 1845-6, bound for Port Essington, 100 miles north-east of modern Darwin, but failed to get even half way. His chief discovery on this trip was a stream he called the Victoria River, which he surmised ran north to the Gulf of Carpentaria. Mitchell was again wrong. In 1847, his deputy leader, Edmund Kennedy, followed Mitchell's river downstream and discovered it to be the upper waters of Sturt's Cooper Creek. The stream was renamed the Barcoo River.

Once again, Mitchell was left with the taste of ashes.

As an explorer, he was something of a drudge, but he kept magnificent journals, meticulous in

Belyando river
Barcoo river
Noqoa
river
Dawson river
Burnett
river
Maranoa river
Condamine river
BRISBANE
MITCHELL 1845-6

detail and copiously illustrated. Many of the drawings were made by professional artists after the expeditions returned to Sydney, from sketches and samples brought back by the explorer. The range of subjects covered in Mitchell's journals includes botany, geology, the aborigines, birds, animals, insects, fish, topography and history. He even makes predictions on the future of the colony though these are unfounded. Most of his subjects are illustrated with drawings, sketches, paintings, maps, lists and tables. Mitchell was a gifted, copious writer with a flair for injecting an atmosphere of adventure into quite ordinary situations. His journals, though somewhat fanciful, are never dull —and they are a rich source of information.

In essence, Major Thomas Livingstone Mitchell was a better chronicler than he was an explorer.

Major Mitchell's fabled "Australia Felix" is today the rich wheat and wool belt of western Victoria. Much of the original mallee scrub has been cleared from the north-western corner of the State, with mixed results. In good seasons, aided by the addition of fertilizers, the sandy country produces excellent cereal crops. After the harvest, sheep graze the remaining stubble. But in dry years, which are common, there is a serious erosion hazard. Red dust storms carry the powdered mallee earth over Melbourne and into New South Wales.

In the richer country discovered by Mitchell now stand some of Victoria's wealthiest towns, including Horsham, Hamilton, Warrnambool and Ballarat. The undulating, well-watered volcanic country centred on the Camperdown area is among the most valuable agricultural and grazing land in Australia. A network of bitumen roads make it possible for modern travellers to duplicate Mitchell's journeys in a matter of days. Among the most impressive monuments to the explorer are the looming grain silos that dot the countryside every few miles.

The high country

Strzelecki and others

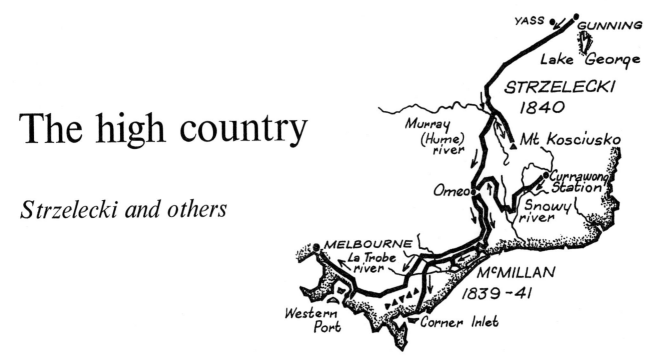

While Major Mitchell was endeavouring to confound Sturt during 1835-6, an insolvent immigrant to Sydney confounded his multitudinous creditors by turning explorer and heading for the Australian Alps. His name was John Lhotsky, a botanist and geologist from Poland who had fled his country to escape Russian reprisals when the 1830 Polish revolt failed.

When he reached Sydney, his only asset was an outstanding gift of the gab, which enabled him to run up a series of bills and talk Governor Bourke into lending him four convicts for a journey of exploration into the alps. He took with him a horse and dray loaded with stores sufficient for three months, all donated or purchased on credit.

In February, 1834, Lhotsky crossed the Canberra Plains, where the national capital now stands, following well-worn tracks between the various sheep stations already established there. Because of his gregarious nature, he seems to have been a popular guest of the local squatters. In his diary, Lhotsky makes no bones about the fact that while he was getting free board and lodgings he was prepared to stay until his welcome wore out.

One of his hosts, Dr Reid, was then in the pro-

cess of shearing 900 sheep on his property called Meneru Plains. He expected to get 15 bales, each weighing 245 lb., from them. Individual blade shearers were handling between 70 and 130 sheep daily. Lhotsky noted that Dr Reid owned a number of properties, his total flocks numbering 2,192. On this, Lhotsky commented darkly: "Our government sells no land except in large parcels, and therefore none to the poor."

Lhotsky's diary consists of a series of rambling dissertations, largely on botanical and geological matters, with a leavening of parish politics. It contains few dates, no maps or measurements and is thoroughly unsatisfactory as a journal of exploration. It does not have the ring of truth about it. Lhotsky's claim to have followed the Snowy River downstream into what is now Victoria is highly suspect. His chief claim to fame seems to be that he discovered a spring of aerated waters near Butong station. He demanded a reward from the Governor for discovering this. When he failed to get it, Lhotsky exposed the fact that a non-existent botanist had been on the government's payroll for some years. Lhotsky demanded the job, and the back pay, but got neither.

In May, 1839, a party set out for Victoria's

39

high country from Currawong station on the upper waters of the Snowy River. It consisted of two men, station overseer Angus McMillan, who had been in the country only three years, and an aboriginal guide, Jimmy Gilbert, who had been in the country all his life.

McMillan was looking for new grazing land for the owner of the station, a fellow Scot named Lachlan Macalister. Local tribesmen had spoken of much good country through the ranges down the river. In a week they had reached the junction with the Buchan River and travelled upstream and north-west into the Omeo district. The country was steep but there was plenty of good grazing land, particularly along the river flats.

When McMillan reported his finds to Macalister, he was sent back immediately to establish a station near the present site of Ensay, on the Tambo River. With two other stockmen, Macalister's son Mathew and an aboriginal guide, McMillan later followed the Tambo to its mouth near what is now Lakes Entrance. Then he travelled farther westward, crossing the Mitchell, Macalister, Thompson and Latrobe rivers, to reach the coast at Corner Inlet, near the present town of Welshpool. This rich grazing country became known as the Gippsland district.

Angus McMillan was delighted with his discoveries and returned to Currawong to write a full and detailed report of his travels to Macalister, who was away in Sydney. The letter was dated 18th February, 1840.

While McMillan was writing his letter, another Polish immigrant was leading an expedition through the alps near by, bound for the country that was the subject of McMillan's report. This party was led by Paul Edmund de Strzelecki, who had been the darling of Sydney society since his arrival in the colony in 1839.

He had discovered extensive gold-fields around Bathurst and Wellington in October, 1839. The Governor, Sir George Gipps, had asked Strzelecki not to publish his news, because he feared the resultant "rush" would leave the colony's 45,000 convicts unguarded. Strzelecki had an engaging personality, like his countryman Lhotsky, and was readily accepted as a scientist, mineralogist, geologist, explorer and bushman. Subsequent events indicated he had little right to the last two titles.

However, he was engaged by two members of the notoriously land-hungry Macarthur and Blax-

land families to examine the south-west corner of Victoria for possible grazing land. Young James Macarthur and John Blaxland had glimpsed this country from a ship when on a trip to Tasmania.

The party consisted of Strzelecki, James Macarthur, an English youth, two convicts and an aboriginal guide. They carried their stores on 6 pack-horses. Starting from Adelong they headed south to the Murray, then travelled upstream into the alps.

From a base camp near what is now Geehi, Strzelecki and Macarthur set out to climb the highest peak they could see. On the second day they feared they might become lost, so Macarthur stayed beside a fire he kept burning while Strzelecki climbed the peak they had chosen. For "bushmen" with compasses in open tundra country with good visibility, this was a remarkably cautious step.

However, Strzelecki returned well after sunset with a piece of rock from the summit of the mountain he called Mt Kosciusko. His map, when compared with a present-day military survey map, indicates that he climbed Mt Ramshead (7,189 ft), which appears to a climber to be as high as, or higher than neighbouring Kosciusko (7,314 ft).

After this detour, the whole party returned downstream to what is now Tintaldra and proceeded along the route of the present Corryong-

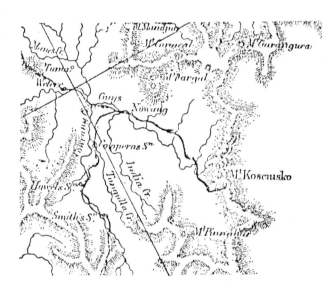

Strzelecki's map shows that he climbed a mountain adjacent to Kosciusko

40

Omeo road. There was apparently a track even then. The travellers reported three stations along the way, before they reached the McFarlane brothers' cattle run near Omeo. The McFarlanes directed Strzelecki and his fellow explorers to a property run by a man named Buckley, or Buckler, who in turn showed them the way to Macalister's station. Two other runs had been established in the area, by settlers named Pender and Hyland. Young Mathew Macalister guided the expedition through the mountains until the rich Gippsland plains were in sight. They were then unnamed.

Left to its own devices, the Strzelecki party was soon in trouble. They lost McMillan's old trail, veered too far inland and were soon enmeshed in dense brush country somewhere above Maffra. Strzelecki was apparently trying to reach Westernport by a conveniently straight course instead of following the open plains country to the south, a longer but easier route. He calculated that Westernport was only 25 miles away, but the distance turned out to be nearer 70 miles.

Instead of backing out of the trouble he had got himself into, as Hume and Hovell had done on the northern side of the range, Strzelecki continued headlong into the brush. Time dragged on, the party sometimes advancing only three miles a day. Food was desperately short. The men resorted to eating raw koala meat when fire lighting became difficult in the damp undergrowth. Their horses were starving. They were abandoned on a small patch of feed. No one liked horsemeat, apparently, for none of the animals was shot for food.

Strzelecki and his men hacked on through the scrub for another 23 days before staggering into an abandoned Westernport settlement. Here they were sheltered and fed by escaped convicts who had occupied the disused buildings after they had been vacated in 1828. It was now 12th May, 1840.

Strzelecki reached Melbourne later in May and wasted no time getting himself into the public eye as the discoverer of vast new tracts of rich grazing land. He named the area Gippsland—after Governor Gipps (who had the amusing eccentricity of not allowing any town to be designed with a public square, because he thought such meeting places encouraged democracy). A Melbourne newspaper acclaimed Strzelecki and the word of his discoveries soon reached Sydney, no doubt to the irritation of his backers, Macarthur and Blaxland.

Unaware of the publicity given to Strzelecki, Angus McMillan opened a stock route from Currawong to the new station at Ensay and on to Port Albert. He and Macalister hoped to keep their discoveries quiet until they had taken up the best of the new land.

McMillan, in particular, was consternated to learn that the whole colony had been told of the new country he was opening up. When he returned along his road to Port Albert, squatters had already arrived by sea and followed his track to take up selections on the plains. He found too that Strzelecki was getting credit for discovering the area.

A public controversy followed, fanned by rival newspapers in Sydney and Melbourne. Eventually McMillan was recognized as the original discoverer of south-eastern Victoria. But his name for the area, Caledonia Australis, was rejected in favour of Strzelecki's title of *Gippsland*.

The distant view of the Australian alps and the adjacent high country of the Monaro and Omeo districts is much the same as in the days of the explorers. Lhotsky, McMillan and Strzelecki would notice few changes.

But the area is no longer inaccessible and forbidding as it once was. There are now good road links between Cooma, Cabramurra, Corryong, Omeo, Bombala and other highland towns. Sealed or well-maintained gravel roads provide tourists with access to the alpine villages and places of interest within the Kosciusko National Park. Lake Eucumbene and various other installations of the Snowy Mountains Scheme draw tourists to the alps throughout the summer months. Chairlifts provide easy access to the top of the ranges. Apart from tourism, sheep and cattle grazing is the basic industry of the highland slopes, from Cooma in New South Wales to the Dargo high plains above Bairnsdale in Victoria.

On the lower reaches of the Snowy River down to Orbost and on the Tambo River below Omeo, graded roads meander through some of Australia's finest scenic country, cleared in places but still basically unspoilt by the hand of man. Of all the Australian continent, these highlands are perhaps the least changed areas since the early days of exploration.

Mount Beadell, on the Gunbarrel highway, through the Gibson Desert

Inhospitable spinifex country in the Hamersley Range, Western Australia. Frank Gregory first examined this now famous mining area, in 1861

The King Leopold Ranges in the Kimberley district of Western Australia. George Grey was first into this area, in 1837

Pine plantations in the Australian Capital Territory. Hume and Hovell skirted westward of the ranges on their 1824 journey to Port Phillip Bay

Saltbush land like this mocked every endeavour of the early inland explorers to find rich country

The waterhole at Depot Glen, where Charles Sturt's expedition was marooned by drought for six months in 1845

Rich grain-growing and grazing country north of Adelaide. Eyre and Stuart were the pioneers of this area

Vineyards south-east of Adelaide. Joseph Hawdon, the first man to overland cattle to Adelaide, passed this way in 1838, followed by Eyre and Sturt

The western coast

Grey and others

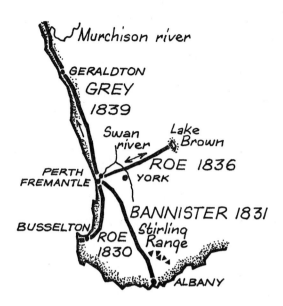

While eastern Victoria was being probed, Joseph Hawdon overlanded the first mob of cattle to the newly established non-convict settlement at Adelaide in 1838. He was followed within months by Sturt, who had decided to settle near Adelaide, and Edward John Eyre, who brought over more stock and hoped to use Adelaide as a base for expeditions into central Australia.

In the same period, exploration of the west coast of the continent began, spurred by a fear that the French or Dutch might establish a footing on the Australian mainland. Port Essington, 100 miles north-east of what is now Darwin, was established in 1824 for similar reasons. The port failed, but was re-occupied in 1838. It was finally abandoned in 1849.

In 1827, Governor Darling sent Major Lockyer to found a penal settlement at King George's Sound, now Albany. It was abandoned after four years. In the same year, Captain James Stirling explored the Swan River where Perth now stands and suggested a settlement. This idea was ignored until another French scare in 1829, when a colony was hastily set up on Garden Island and later the banks of the Swan River. Perth was officially gazetted as a town in August 1829.

The following year, the surveyor-general of the new colony, Captain John Septimus Roe, explored

south along the coast to Bunbury and Busselton, where a few families settled. Thomas Bannister travelled overland to King George's Sound in 1831, then exploration lapsed for several years.

The isolated colony languished, its population dwindling from 4,000 to 1,500 in the mid-1830s.

Interest in the west coast revived slightly in 1837. A sea-borne exploration party, led by Captain George Grey, arrived on the Kimberley coast direct from England, via Cape Town. Grey and all but one of his 12-man party had never been to Australia. They planned to walk overland to Perth! The impossibility of this task became apparent after they came ashore, and Grey sensibly contented himself with various small excursions inland.

He landed initially with his 11 men and 31 sheep, 19 goats and six dogs, plus a variety of seeds and seedling trees. While Grey and his party established a garden and observed such interesting local phenomena as walking fish and green tailor ants, their ship sailed away to Timor, to return with 26 ponies, another 14 sheep, coconut and breadfruit trees.

The explorers started their first excursion on 17th December, 1837. The local tribesmen, apparently used to fighting with Malayan intruders, proved extremely aggressive. Grey made every

c

endeavour to get along peaceably with them and was badly speared for his pains. In self-defence, he shot one attacker.

Despite his wounds, he scouted the country in various directions until 17th April, penetrating about 70 miles inland. He discovered and named the Glenelg River, which he followed up toward the King Leopold Ranges.

There, on the eastern slopes of a range to the east of the river, Grey made a startling discovery. He found a series of unusual cave paintings: large mouthless figures, each with a head surmounted by a glowing halo, stared down at the explorers from the roofs and walls of several caves. The mysterious paintings were unlike any other aboriginal work discovered before or since in Australia.

For many years it was supposed they were of Malay origin, or the work of some unknown visitors from the sea. But they are now regarded as aboriginal in origin. Known as Wondjina figure paintings, they were inspired by distant aboriginal memories of voyagers who reached the Kimberley coast perhaps many centuries ago. Just who these visitors were remains a mystery.

The Wondjina people, according to aboriginal legend, roamed the Kimberleys for some time. When their journeys ended, the marks of their bodies remained on the walls of the caves where they had lived. Their spirits, which the aborigines associated with rain and natural increase, went to live in near-by pools. These benevolent spirits could be invoked when the "bodies" of the Wondjina were repainted. The aborigines had done this for generations before Grey arrived.

The explorers left the Kimberley coast in mid-April, 1837, and sailed for the island of Mauritius, where Grey recovered from his spear wounds.

The party eventually sailed to Perth. Late in 1838 and during 1839, Grey explored much of the coast between Shark Bay and Perth, walking some of the way but rarely penetrating more than a few miles inland. There was more trouble with warlike aborigines and on one journey supplies ran short and one man died of hunger.

Grey made no significant discoveries, but he added considerably to the knowledge of the west Australian coast.

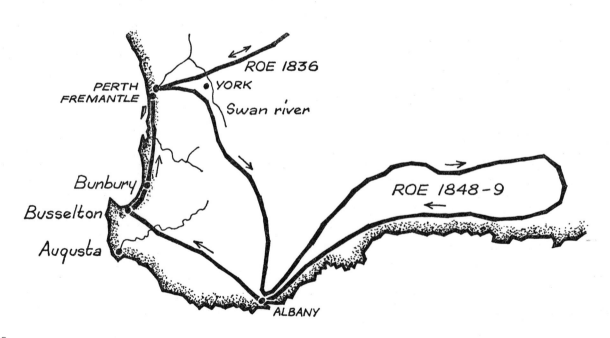

The state of the colony—1840

When Grey arrived in Perth, which was still in the doldrums, the Colony of Australia was 50 years old. Hawdon, Sturt and Eyre had arrived in the burgeoning colony of South Australia. Moreton Bay, established as a penal settlement in 1824, had so far not attracted many free settlers.

Melbourne, set up illegally in 1835 under the guidance of Batman and Fawkner, had been officially recognized in 1836 and was booming. By 1840, the population was 20,000. A score of un-official settlements were located along the New South Wales and Victorian coasts, established by whalers and sealers from various countries such as America, or by farming families like the Hentys at Portland (1834) and the Bussels at Busselton (1830), south of Perth.

Cattle and sheep runs extended inland from Sydney for several hundred miles in all directions. A few settlers were as far afield as New England and the Darling Downs. There were a number of stations in the eastern Riverina and on the Monaro high plains. There were already half a dozen stations on what was to become the Victorian side of the alps and the name Gippsland was soon to be on everyone's lips.

Cattle and sheep runs straddled the Murrumbidgee and the Murray for some miles west of the Sydney-Melbourne road.

There was a thriving settlement at Geelong by 1838 and a handful of squatters probing north-west into Major Mitchell's fabled Australia Felix. Settlers were already at the mouth of the Glenelg River, west of Portland, taking up land for sheep grazing.

In 1836, Governor Bourke had decreed that anyone could squat on Crown lands for a yearly payment of £10 as a squatting licence. The squatter had no right of ownership to the land and could be turned off when his licence expired.

The free settlers and emancipists (freed convicts) who took up holdings worked their properties with the aid of convict labour. They were obliged to feed and clothe the convicts, thus saving the British Government this expense, but did not pay wages. Under threat of being returned to the chain gangs of Sydney or the dungeons of Van Diemen's Land, the convicts worked reasonably well.

Assigned convict Henry Tingley wrote home in 1835: ". . . All a man has got to mind is keep a still tongue in his head, and do his master's duty . . . but if he don't he may as well be hung at once, for they would take you to the magistrates and get 100 of lashes, and then get sent to a place called Port Arthur to work in irons for two or three years."

Life in the bush was hard, for free settlers and convicts alike. Roads were almost non-existent and even the well-used tracks were difficult and sometimes dangerous, particularly in wet weather. There were few bridges—creeks and rivers had to be forded. Bushrangers were out in places and presented another hazard.

Overlanders with cattle had to be on guard

against local settlers who "rushed" their herds at night in an attempt to run off a few beasts for themselves.

Finding a new run in the 1830s and 1840s became a minor feat of exploration. Intending settlers had to push out beyond the occupied runs, locate grass and water and then get their stock there before someone else jumped their claims. Fences, except those round homestead yards, were almost unknown. A squatter marked the boundaries of his property with a few scarfed trees and protected his empire with stockwhip and gun.

Stores and equipment for the setting up of a new run were hauled on bullock drays. A pioneer squatter, Edmund Morey, wrote: "As a rule, the man intending to take and stock new country started with cattle and sufficient number of horses to serve for two or three years . . . The intending pioneer . . . got his teams ready, and laid in supplies of various kinds and other requisites for the buildings necessary on a new station . . .

"The rations used up-country were simple . . . Tea, generally in 84-lb. chests, commonly called 'post and rails'—from its coarse quality—was the usual ration tea, and dark brown sugar from Mauritius . . . This same treacly-looking sugar would, in the dry climate of the west, become so hard as to need breaking with a tomahawk. The flour served out was wholesome and more sustaining than the extremely fine white product of the present day (about 1907), but it was apt to become weevily if kept too long; the weight was 200 pounds, put up in such substantial bags as to keep the flour from hurt if exposed to rain.

"Niggerhead tobacco and short clay pipes always formed part of our outfit . . . Our cooking utensils were not numerous: just a camp oven for baking meat and bread, an iron pot for boiling meat or vegetables—if we had any—quartpot and pint pots, a couple of cans for water, a big tin or iron dish for meat, with a large iron fork and big butcher's knife for carving, constituted the usual outfit . . ."

George Hamilton, one of the early settlers along the Murray River in the 1840s, described the building of a squatter's hut. "Near a long waterhole fringed with reeds several huts were erected: they were built of bark stripped from stringy-bark trees growing in the forests that clothed the neighbouring hills. These sheets of bark were stretched out and tied by strings of green bullock hide to a framework composed of saplings, tied together with strings of similar nature. The whole structure was made of stringybark and greenhide —walls, roof and chimney; not a nail was used in the entire building . . . Inside the fireplace, which was large enough to contain many persons, stones were built up against the bark to prevent the latter igniting. Bark shelves resting on wooden pegs ran around the walls."

Nails were in short supply in those days, as were horse-shoes and other metal items.

Although life was hard for the early explorers and settlers, it was hardest of all for the displaced aborigines. With some exceptions, most settlers hunted them off their properties like animals. In the early days it was assumed that a tribe displaced from one area could settle down and hunt on neighbouring land without friction with the aborigines already living in that area. But the tribes had a very strong sense of territory and there was usually bloodshed when one group was prodded onto another's territory. There was usually insufficient game and fish for two tribes in the same area, particularly when the white men began to net the streams for fish and systematically shoot kangaroos, koalas and possums for the skin trade.

Deprived of their traditional game, the aborigines speared the white man's sheep and cattle— which led to harsh reprisals.

Whole tribes were wiped out in a matter of days or weeks in some areas, long before the arrival of law and order or official chroniclers of district history. Few pioneers were proud enough of these early massacres to speak or write of them. Some did. An early settler of the Portland area wrote: ". . . Three days after the Whytes arrived, the natives of this creek, with some others, made up a plan to rob the newcomers, as they had done Messrs. Henty before.

"They waited an opportunity, and cut off 50 sheep from Whyte brothers' flock, which were soon missed and the natives followed; they had taken shelter in an open plain with a long clump of tea-tree, which the Whyte brothers' party, seven in number, surrounded, and shot them all but one. Fifty-one men were killed, and the bones of the men and sheep lay mingled together bleaching in the sun . . ."

In 1843, the Governor of South Australia heard a speaker at a meeting of that colony's Missionary Society tell of atrocities committed against the aborigines, which concluded thus: ". . . they were being shot down in mistake for native dogs, and their bleeding and ghastly heads had been exhibited on poles, as scare-crows to their fellows."

In the year 1840, while Strzelecki and McMillan were arguing about who was first to discover the rich grazing lands of eastern Victoria, Edward John Eyre set out from Adelaide for the centre of Australia.

In that year, public antagonism to the convict transport system brought results and it was declared that no more felons would be shipped to New South Wales. The squatters, who depended on cheap labour, objected, but the rest of the community rejoiced.

There were then 101,000 free citizens and 27,000 convicts in the colony. Land, where it could be bought, was selling for around £1 an acre.

The Governors of the colony had been:

Captain Arthur Phillip	1788-1792
Captain John Hunter	1795-1800
Captain Philip King	1800-1806
Captain William Bligh	1806-1808
Major-General Lachlan Macquarie	1810-1821
Major-General Sir Thomas Brisbane	1821-1825
Lieutenant General Ralph Darling	1825-1831
Major-General Sir Richard Bourke	1831-1837
Sir George Gipps	1838-1846

When Phillip arrived with the First Fleet, the Colony of New South Wales extended from Cape York to Wilson's Promontory and westward to the 135th degree of longitude (about 70 miles east of Alice Springs). In 1803, Van Diemen's Land was annexed. In 1825, the western boundary of New South Wales was shifted to the present boundary with Western Australia. Four years later, in 1829, possession was taken of Western Australia, making the entire continent British.

Although Britain claimed sovereignty over what was the world's largest island and the world's smallest continent, little was known of the nearly three-million-square-miles hinterland bounded by the colony's 12,210 miles of coastline. Most of the interior had yet to be explored.

Into the silence

Eyre

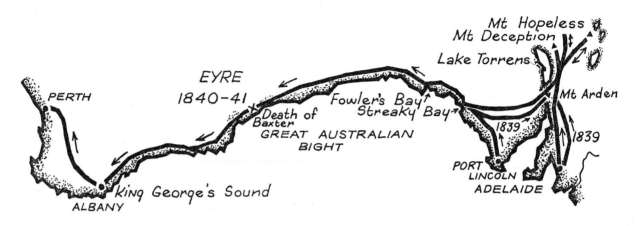

"Mr. Eyre goes forth this day, to endeavour to plant the British flag . . . on the tropic of Capricorn, as nearly as possible in 135 or 136 degrees of longitude, in the very centre of our island continent . . ."—*Governor Gawler on the occasion of Eyre's departure, 18th June, 1840.*

Before this expedition, Eyre had been the second man to overland stock to Melbourne (1837) and to Adelaide (1838), being a close second to Joseph Hawdon on both occasions. In trying to beat Hawdon to Adelaide, he pushed his cattle through Victoria's dry mallee country, discovering Lake Hindmarsh. Then dry country forced him north to Hawdon's longer, safer route along the Murray River.

Finding a hungry market for stock in Adelaide, Eyre sailed back immediately to Sydney. He arrived there on 2nd October and on the 17th was bound for Adelaide once more, with 600 cattle, 1,000 sheep, two drays, two carts, 10 horses, 14 working bullocks and 16 men. Eyre's zeal and enterprise were rewarded 14 weeks later, when he arrived safely in Adelaide and became the first

man to overland sheep to the new colony. He was then only 24 years of age.

He bought a small property in Adelaide, but in May, 1839 went exploring northward as far as Mt Arden at the head of Spencer Gulf. Dry country stopped him. On 29th, Eyre was home in Adelaide and nine days later went aboard a ship bound for Port Lincoln. He wanted to explore the country west of Spencer Gulf and perhaps find an overland stock route to Western Australia. His companions, as before, were John Baxter and two aboriginal youths.

Beyond Streaky Bay, dry country again stopped him, so he made his way overland to the head of Spencer Gulf, the termination of his previous trip, and returned to Adelaide. In January of the following year, 1840, he took a boat-load of sheep and some cattle to Albany and overlanded them to the Perth district, following a route pioneered by Thomas Bannister in 1831.

Not long after his return to Adelaide, Eyre decided to try again to penetrate northward into the secret heart of the continent. It was then 1st June, 1840. By 18th June, the expedition was on its way.

In 17 days, Eyre had sold up his property and belongings, purchased horses, saddles and other equipment, hired men, raised money by public subscription and obtained a small government grant for his project.

In round figures, the expedition cost £1,300, raised as follows:

Government donation: £100
Donations by colonists: £580
Amount paid by Eyre: £680

Eyre's companions were five white men and two young aboriginal youths. Concerning his plans, he wrote: "We had with us 13 horses and 40 sheep, and our other stores were calculated for about three months; in addition to which we were to have a further supply forwarded to the head of Spencer's Gulf by sea . . . This would give us the means of remaining out nearly six months, if we found the country practicable, and in that time we might, if no obstacles intervened, easily reach the centre of the Continent and return, or if practicable, cross to Port Essington on the North West coast."

It was not to be. Moving almost due north from the head of Spencer Gulf, Eyre encountered the boggy eastern shore of Lake Torrens. The country became progressively more desolate and waterless. At one point he approached the shoreline of Lake Eyre south, but mistook it for a continuation of Lake Torrens.

Convinced there was an impassable salt lake to the west and the north, he headed east, to be confronted by what appeared to be a continuous shoreline of low salt bogs. He was in fact confounded by three separate lakes: Lake Blanche, Lake Callabonna and Lake Frome. This sandy country is among the most inhospitable territory in Australia. The hardships endured by Eyre and his men were savage in the extreme.

There was little or no feed for the horses and water could be obtained only after digging in dry creek beds. The small band of aborigines Eyre met were having water troubles too. The explorer noted one group carrying a supply in two kangaroo skins, ". . . each containing six to eight quarts; it was quite muddy and had evidently been taken from a puddle in the plains . . ."

Mirages bedevilled Eyre. Near the northern tip of Lake Torrens, he wrote: "Crossing the sandy ridge bounding the basin of the lake, I was surprised to see its bed apparently much contracted, and the opposite shore distinctly visible, high, rocky and bluff to the edge of the water, seemingly only seven or eight miles distant, and with several small islands or rocks scattered over its surface. This was however only deceptive, and caused by the very refractive state of the atmosphere at the time, for upon dismounting and leading the horses into the bed of the lake, the opposite shore appeared to recede, and the rocks or islands turned out to be only very small lumps of dirt or clay lying on the bed of the lake . . .

"I penetrated into the basin of the lake for about six miles, and found it so far without surface water. On entering at first, the horses sunk a little in a stiff mud, after breaking through a white crust of salt . . . as we advanced the mud became much softer and greatly mixed with salt water below the surface, until at last we found it impossible to advance a step further, as the horses had already sunk up to their bellies . . .

"Could we have gone on for some distance, I have no doubt that we should have found the bed of the lake occupied by water, as there was every appearance of a large body of it to the west. As we advanced a great alteration had taken place, in the aspect of the western shores. The bluff rocky banks were no longer visible, but a low level country appeared to the view at seemingly about 15 or 20 miles distance. From the extraordinary and deceptive appearances, caused by mirage and refraction, however, it was impossible to tell what to make of sensible objects, or what to believe on the evidence of vision, for upon turning back to retrace our steps to the eastward, a vast sheet of water appeared to intervene between us and the shore, whilst the Mount Deception ranges, which I knew to be at least 35 miles distant, seemed to rise out of the bed of the lake itself . . ."

Heading eastward, Eyre was confronted again by a seemingly continuous shoreline of salt bogs. Finally, tortured by thirst and hunger, he turned back at a hill he named Mt Hopeless, which stands between lakes Blanche and Callabonna.

When the party retreated to the head of Spencer Gulf, near the present site of Port Augusta, Eyre and his men had recovered some strength and spirit. Instead of admitting defeat and returning to Adelaide, Eyre split the party, sending one group under Baxter to follow his 1839 route to Streaky Bay. Eyre led the rest of his expedition down the west coast of the Gulf to Port Lincoln.

53

There he obtained further supplies, after sending one of his men in a small chartered craft across to Adelaide. A government ship, the *Waterwitch*, brought the goods over. Eyre arranged to rendez-vous with the *Waterwitch* at Streaky Bay, where he rejoined Baxter and the rest of his men.

The expedition then headed westward along the shoreline, bound for the colony of Western Australia. The Governor of South Australia had originally wanted Eyre to probe in this direction, but the explorer had caused him to change his mind. Now, after his chastening experiences in the Lake Torrens basin, Eyre was apparently glad to change *his* plans. He had previously told the Governor, on the basis of his journey to Streaky Bay in 1839, that an overland route to the west was impossible. But Eyre, the impetuous young man who liked to be first in his chosen fields of endeavour, apparently decided it would be better to be remembered as the first man to cross the continent from east to west than as the first man to fail in his efforts to cross from south to north.

Eyre was immediately in trouble west of Streaky Bay. The scrub was so thick in places it had to be cleared with axes to make way for the drays. There was little grazing for the horses and the only water available had to be dug for in the sand dunes, sometimes to a depth of 15 feet. The *Waterwitch* rendezvoused with the party at Smoky Bay, Denial Bay and Fowler's Bay, bringing up kegs of drinking water and other supplies for the men.

Noting that he and his men would have perished without the supplies they carried and the assistance of the *Waterwitch*, Eyre remarked on the fact that the aborigines in the area seemed to live well despite the wretchedness of the country. They, he pointed out, "followed us on foot, keeping up in a line with the dray through the scrub and procuring their food as they went along, which consisted of snakes, lizards, guanas, bandicoots, rats, wallabies, &c. &c. and it was surprising to see the apparent ease with which, in merely walking across the country, they each procured an abundant supply for the day."

Aboriginal guides showed Eyre the location of several rock waterholes and wells dug in the sand. Eyre unstintingly acknowledged their invaluable assistance, on his travels. He wrote: ". . . without their guidance, we could never have removed from any encampment without previously ascertaining where the next water could be procured;

and to have done this would have caused us great delay, and much additional toil. By having them with us we were enabled to move with confidence and celerity; and in following their guidance we knew that we were taking that line of route which was the shortest and the best practicable under the circumstances. Upon arriving at any of the watering places to which they had conducted us, they always pointed out the water and gave it to us entirely, no longer looking upon it as their own and literally not taking a drink from it themselves when thirsty without first asking permission from us. Surely this true politeness—this genuine hospitality of the untutored savage, may well put to the blush, for their exclusiveness and illiberality, his more civilised brethren . . ."

At Fowler's Bay, Eyre found many signs that whalers had been camping in the area. In his journal he pointed out that no British ships were engaged in this profitable trade, though some 300 French and American whalers were said to be operating out of the southern ports of Australia. Eyre was surprised to find the shell of a very large turtle on the beach in Fowler's Bay. He wrote that it ". . . could not have weighed less than three to four hundredweight. I was not previously aware that turtle was ever found so far to the southward, and had never seen the least trace of them before."

On 17th December, Eyre sent two of his men back to Adelaide in the *Waterwitch*, together with a request for a supply of oats and bran for the starving horses. He also announced his plan to press on round the coastline to Albany in King George's Sound.

During the one month wait for the return of the ship, Eyre, Baxter and two aboriginal youths reconnoitred westward over 100 miles before being forced back through lack of water. On 26th January, the cutter *Hero* sailed into Fowler's Bay, having replaced the *Waterwitch*, on the Governor's instructions. She brought supplies of oats and bran for the horses and a friendly suggestion from the Governor that Eyre should give up his plan to push westward and confine himself to explorations within South Australia. The Governor pointed out that the *Hero* could not be used outside South Australian waters.

Eyre wrote: ". . . the plan I had formed of sending our drays and heavy stores in her to Cape Arid, whilst we proceeded overland ourselves with pack-horses, was completely over-turned."

Major Mitchell talks with aborigines at the Murray River on his 1836 expedition

"Natives dance at the report of a pistol"—the caption to this drawing in Mitchell's journal. There was bloodshed between Mitchell and the aborigines on most of his journeys

Overleaf: Quartz country surrounding Depot Glen, where Sturt and his men were trapped by drought for six months in 1845

On Kosciusko's slopes, the high country first approached by John Lhotsky in 1834 and visited by Paul Edmund Strzelecki in 1840

Mallee scrub of the kind encountered by Sturt, Mitchell and Eyre in north-west Victoria in the 1830s

Instead, Eyre decided to reduce his party to the absolute minimum. He would push on with the two aboriginal youths and another, called Wylie, who had arrived aboard the *Hero*. Wylie had previously travelled overland with Eyre between Perth and Albany and returned with him on the ship to Adelaide.

Eyre had sent a letter from Port Lincoln to Adelaide, asking that Wylie be sent to join him. Wylie was a native of the Albany district and Eyre anticipated that he would be useful as a guide and interpreter should his expedition press so far westward. The idea of getting through to Albany must have been strong in Eyre's mind while he was in Port Lincoln.

Eyre makes it clear in his journal that he knew what hardships lay ahead of him beyond Fowler's Bay. He knew from recent personal experience that there was scant stock feed and no surface water for the next 100 miles. Beyond that, Eyre's copy of Matthew Flinders's chart of the coastline showed hundreds of miles of steep cliffs, with little possibility of feed or water. About midway across the Bight, sandhills where water might be obtained were indicated. But the chart also indicated dense scrub that would probably force any land traveller to walk almost at the ocean's edge. No open grassy country was shown.

Clearly Eyre knew full well that he would have to follow virtually within a stone's throw of the shore for most of his journey, discovering nothing that had not already been recorded by passing ships. Why did he press on, when failure seemed inevitable, there was nothing to be discovered, and his erstwhile supporters had requested him to return to Adelaide?

A blind, fanatical stubbornness to be the first man to achieve something truly monumental and unforgettable seems to be the only answer.

Eyre's confidence was somewhat infectious. His faithful overseer, John Baxter, chose to remain with him when the little party on the beach watched the *Hero* sail away on the evening of 30th January, 1841. For a month the two white men and three aboriginal youngsters lingered at Fowler's Bay, while the horses grew daily stronger on their rations of oats and bran.

On 24th February, as Eyre, Baxter and the three aborigines were preparing to leave, the *Hero* returned to Fowler's Bay from Adelaide. A letter from the Governor requested Eyre to return on the *Hero* and continue his explorations within the colony. Eyre wrote a polite refusal and set off westward.

Eyre recorded: "The party consisted of myself, the overseer, three native boys, nine horses, one Timor pony, one foal, born at Streaky Bay, and six sheep; our flour . . . was calculated for nine weeks, at an allowance of six pounds of flour each weekly, with a proportionate quantity of tea and sugar."

In the first week, the 850-mile summer journey developed into a nightmare of heat, flies, thirst, hunger and uncertainty. Shade temperatures reached 113 degrees. Every drop of water had to be dug for. The horses starved and knocked up.

Several times they were without water for five days, a seemingly impossible feat of endurance for loaded animals in summer weather. The men found drinking water by soaking up morning dew in sponges and squeezing it into quart pots. At one stage, Eyre recorded of the horses: "They had been seven days without a drop of water, and almost without food also . . ."

The great centralian explorer, Ernest Giles, who used horses extensively on his travels over a period of many years, openly doubted Eyre's claim. He wrote sarcastically: "This journey of Eyre's was very remarkable in more ways than one; its most extraordinary incident being the statement that his horses travelled for seven days and nights without water. I have travelled with horses in almost every part of Australia, but I know that after three days and three nights without water horses would certainly knock up, die, or become utterly useless, and it would be impossible to make them continue travelling . . ."

The overseer Baxter became despondent and requested Eyre several times to turn back. Eyre recorded this a number of times in his journal, with his opinion that Baxter had caused the aboriginal youngsters to lose heart also. "They had imbibed the overseer's idea that we never should succeed in our attempt to get to the westward . . ."

Wylie and the elder of the two South Australian youths deserted for several days. This was a most unusual liaison, between two aborigines from widely separated parts of the continent and having no common language between them. Eyre reported them back, hungry and sullen, after four days.

Another four days found the starving, tension-ridden party camped on flat rocky country above a second line of cliffs they had encountered. From his chart showing the 100-mile line of cliffs, Eyre would have known there was little possibility of finding water for another seven days at their usual rate of travel. They were already three days from the last water and had five gallons left.

This amount would never sustain five men tramping in the heat of summer for the next seven days.

That night, Eyre's journal records, the two South Australian youths shot Baxter and absconded with a gallon-keg of water, 20 pounds of baked bread, "some mutton, tea and sugar, Baxter's tobacco and pipes, some clothes, two double-barrelled guns, some ammunition, and a few other small articles".

Eyre, who had been watching the horses in the darkness, was on the scene within five minutes of hearing the fatal shot fired. But this was sufficient time, apparently, for the two youthful desperadoes to make off with their considerable load of booty. Lacking haversacks or a pack-horse, it is not clear how they carried these goods.

Next morning, Eyre and Wylie continued sadly on, leaving the body of the overseer wrapped in a blanket on the flat rocky surface above the cliffs. There was nowhere to dig a grave to which some later party might have come for the purpose of retrieving the poor man's bones for burial in Adelaide.

It was providential for Eyre that his party was reduced from five to two persons at a time when there were only five gallons of water left for an expected dry stage of seven days!

Eyre recorded sighting the two aboriginal youths next day, but they were never seen again and perhaps died in the desert. Three days later, Eyre and Wylie were overjoyed to find a native well in the sand dunes at the end of the line of cliffs. Travelling sometimes by moonlight, they had covered more than 30 miles on some days. Once again, the horses had performed the astounding feat of going seven days and seven nights without water, travelling 150 miles westward in the process!

A further 150 miles brought Eyre and Wylie to a snug cove where by a miraculous stroke of luck they found a French whaling ship anchored. The captain, an Englishman named Rossiter, sheltered and fed the explorers on board for a fortnight while they recovered their strength. In his gratitude, Eyre named the cove Rossiter Bay. Then, well provisioned by the generous captain, he and Wylie struggled on to Albany. From there they followed the overland route to Perth which Eyre had travelled previously.

The continent had been crossed from east to west and Eyre was for a time the toast of the colonies. But he had discovered nothing of any value. The work for which he should be most admired came later. After his return to Adelaide, he was appointed Protector of Aborigines on the Murray River.

His work in this field was outstanding. Eyre probably did more than any other man toward improving understanding between black and white Australians. He was one of the first Europeans to achieve any real understanding of the aboriginal way of life, to earn their confidence and respect and to actively champion their cause.

His 350-page study, *Manners and Customs of the Aborigines of Australia* remains as one of the most humane, thoughtful and conscience-stirring documents on Aborigines. As an explorer, Eyre achieved little and enjoyed only a brief moment of fame. But he will be remembered as a great champion of the aborigines and the author of what might be described as the first charter of aboriginal rights.

Towards the dead heart

Sturt

"Poole has just returned from the ranges . . . He says that there are high ranges to N. and N.W. and water—a sea extending along the horizon . . . in which there are a number of islands . . . Tomorrow we start for the ranges, and then for the waters—the strange waters on which boat never swam, and over which flag never floated. But both shall ere long. We have the heart of the interior laid open to us, and shall be off with a flowing sheet in a few days. Poole says that the sea was a deep blue, and that in the midst of it there was a conical island of great height. When will you hear from me again?"—*Captain Charles Sturt in a private letter to a friend in Adelaide, dated 14th October, 1844.*

For three years following Eyre's return from the west, no major attempt was made from any of the colonies to penetrate to the centre of the continent. Captain Charles Sturt was the next man to try. Like Eyre, he had come overland from New South Wales to live in South Australia. Unlike Eyre, he still believed in the possibility of an inland sea or lake somewhere near the centre of the continent.

He set out from Adelaide in August, 1844. It was 14 years since his great voyage of discovery down the Murray. Sturt was approaching 50 years of age

and knew that he had not many years left to realize his long cherished ambition of being the first man to reach the centre of the Australian continent.

From his own observations and through studying the journals of other travellers, he had formed the opinion that Australia had once been an archipelago—a chain of islands. The continent, he surmised, had been elevated, draining the sea from what were now the inland plains and salt bogs. "I am still of opinion that there is more than one sea in the interior of the Australian continent, but such may not be the case" he wrote before setting out in 1844.

Sturt was approximately right in his theory about the geological history of Australia, though of course in his time there was no inland sea.

On 10th August, 1844 his government-financed expedition set out on what was to be a monumental feat of endurance. Sturt had 15 men in his party. James Poole was second in command and John McDouall Stuart was the expedition draftsman. There was also a surgeon, a storekeeper, a collector, two servants, a stockman, a horseman, a sheepman, four bullock drivers and one sailor. The caravan included one boat and carriage, one horse dray, one spring cart, three bullock drays, 11 horses, 30 bullocks, 200 sheep, four kangaroo dogs and two sheep dogs.

61

The expedition reached the home of Sturt's "excellent friend", Edward John Eyre, at Moorundie (near present-day Blanchetown) on the Murray on 17th August. Eyre had been Protector of Aborigines for several years and had travelled up the Darling as far as Laidley's Ponds (now Menindie). He had completely won the confidence of the local aborigines and had two guides waiting for Sturt.

While travelling to Laidley's Ponds, Sturt heard stories from local aborigines of a recent battle with white men. Tribesmen had ambushed some sleeping overlanders and killed 15, stealing their stores and clothes. Sturt proceeded cautiously, expecting to come upon a "sad scene of butchery". But further inquiries indicated that the stories referred to the battle with Major Mitchell and his party, eight years earlier!

Guided from waterhole to waterhole by his aboriginal helpers, Sturt pushed north-west through what is now Broken Hill to a point now called Brougham's Gate, near the border between South Australia and New South Wales.

He sent Poole and another man reconnoitring towards Eyre's Mt Hopeless, near Lake Callabonna. They reached Yandama Creek, encountering shallow, brackish lakes, swamps and sandy ridges. There was no grass and the water was difficult to reach across the bogs and would soon dry up. (There had been considerable rain in the past weeks.) After a fortnight, Poole returned to Sturt's base camp. At first Sturt thought Poole had reached the shoreline of an inland sea, but he eventually realized that Poole had been looking at the salt lakes that had stopped Eyre several years earlier.

It was now early December and the summer heat became intense. Shade temperatures of 125 degrees were recorded and the thermometer rarely showed less than 96 degrees. Poole brought back one encouraging item of information. Near the shallow temporary lakes, he had flushed immense numbers of bitterns, cranes and other aquatic birds. Sturt noted: "Whence could these birds have come from? To what quarter do they go? They do not frequent the Murray or the Darling in such numbers, neither do they frequent the southern portion of the coast. If then they are not to be found in these localities, what waters do they inhabit in the interior?"

Sturt sent his stockman, Robert Flood, due north to scout for water. A large supply was needed—Sturt estimated the daily requirements of his stock at not less than 1,000 gallons. Small native soaks and rock holes, or shallow rain pools were of little use to him. In his journal, Sturt several times noted that his otherwise reliable aboriginal guides sometimes deliberately led him past waterholes that he later discovered independently. He expressed disappointment and puzzlement at this seemingly "treacherous" behaviour. It apparently never dawned on this otherwise thoughtful traveller that the loss of a waterhole to thirsty cattle and horses could mean death to local aborigines dependent on it as their only supply.

Flood discovered long deep pools of water in a rocky creek bed 40 miles to the north and Sturt quickly moved up and established a new base. The recent rains had brought up good feed for the animals and Sturt described them as "up to their knees in luxuriant vegetation".

He went on to report: "We there found a native wheat, a beautiful oat, and a rye, as well as a variety of grasses; and in hollows on the plains a blue or purple vetch (parakeelya) not unusual on the sand ridges, of which the cattle were very fond . . . I was surprised that the country was not better inhabited than it appeared to be; for however unfit for civilized man, it seemed a most desirable one for the savage, for there was no want of game of the larger kind, as emus and kangaroos, whilst in every tree and bush there was a nest of some kind or other, and a variety of vegetable productions of which these rude people are fond. Yet we saw no more than six or seven natives . . ."

The aborigines knew the country better than Sturt. This brief green flush, brought on by summer storms, would shrivel to dust in a few months' time and the migratory wildlife would disappear over the horizon, in search of greener pastures. Only a desert would remain.

Sturt sent Poole and John Browne to the north to scout for water. Sturt reconnoitred eastward with Flood and McDouall Stuart. They returned after several days without having located any worthwhile waterholes. It was now 18th December. Sturt wrote: "The heat now became so great that it was almost unbearable, the thermometer rose every day to 112 or 116 degrees in the shade, whilst in the direct rays of the sun from 140 to 150 degrees."

Flood went out scouting for water but returned

unsuccessful on Christmas day. A few hours later, Poole and Browne returned, having been absent for fourteen days. They had travelled almost to the 28th parallel (the present New South Wales-Queensland border) and discovered deep rocky waterholes.

The summer heat was like an inferno. Sturt feared his bullocks and horses would knock up if he tried to push on. He waited until 28th December, when a cool southerly dropped temperatures. Then the cavalcade moved off. For a weary month they plodded northward, stopping at various camps for several days to recuperate and scout ahead for water. Many of the large waterholes located by Poole and Browne had shrunk to a fraction of their former size.

Some drays had to be temporarily abandoned as the bullocks knocked up. When the men returned for them with fresh animals a few days later, they found that some of the waterholes they had used earlier were now completely dry.

Fortunately, the largest waterhole discovered by Poole and Browne seemed to have held its depth during the blazing month since they had first seen it. It was located amid green shady trees at the base of a cliff in a rocky glen. Sturt established a base camp here on 27th January, 1845, calling it Depot Glen. The explorer recorded in his journal: "We pitched our tents . . . little imagining that we were destined to remain at that lonely spot for six weary months. We were not then aware that our advance and our retreat were alike cut off."

In the following months, while their strength and spirits sagged, Sturt and small groups of his men probed to every point of the compass in search of water and grass. They found a few small pools, but no stock feed. Sturt came unwittingly close to success on 13th February, when with Stuart he penetrated north to within 15 miles of Cooper Creek, where there were many long, deep, and permanent waterholes, well stocked with fish and wildfowl. But it is doubtful whether he could have brought his main party this distance, 150 miles, considering the weak state of his bullocks and horses, and the almost complete lack of water along the route. Shade temperatures rose to 132 degrees; in the sun the thermometer recorded 157 degrees! Sturt and his men suffered violent headaches, their skin remained bone dry, the sweat evaporating as it formed. The horses stood motionless, heads low to the ground, tails trembling.

Time dragged on and the water level at Depot Glen receded. The large and varied bird population migrated to the north-west, strengthening Sturt's opinion that a large mass of water must lie in that direction. Some of the men became ill with scurvy and other ailments. James Poole lapsed into a serious condition and was confined to his tent.

Sturt and his men probed in all directions, but could find no better country. The occasional aboriginal families they encountered at small waterholes were small in stature and in a miserable condition. They appeared to Sturt to be much poorer specimens of humanity than the strapping Darling River tribes-people.

The explorer wrote: "It was not however until after we had run down every creek in our neighbourhood, and had traversed the country in every direction, that the truth flashed across my mind, and it became evident to me, that we were locked up in the desolate and heated region, into which we had penetrated, as effectually as if we had wintered at the Pole."

On one of these excursions, men and horses were without water for two days, then came to a boggy waterhole. Sturt wrote. ". . . the mud in the creek was so thick that I could not swallow it, and was really astonished how Mr. Browne managed to drink a pint of it made into tea. It absolutely fell over the cup of the pannikin like thick cream, and stuck to the horses' noses like pipe-clay."

An old aborigine came to Depot Glen and stayed two weeks. He appeared to know the use for which Sturt's boat was intended and pointed to the north-west as the way it should be taken.

"It appeared quite clear to us that he was aware of the existence of large water somewhere or other to the northward and westward", Sturt wrote. "He . . . explained that large waves higher than his head broke on the shore. On my shewing him the fish figured in Sir Thomas Mitchell's work he knew only the cod. Of the fish figured in Cuvier's works he gave specific names to those he recognised . . ."

Sturt was greatly heartened by the old man's news and looked forward to the day when rain would enable him to push into the north-west. Obviously, the inland sea was near at hand. The old man left the camp and was never seen again. May and June came and went. Storm clouds appeared frequently in the sky, but there was scarcely a drop of rain.

63

Sturt recorded: "A gloomy silence pervaded the camp . . . We had gradually been deserted by every beast of the field, and every fowl of the air. We had witnessed migration after migration of the feathered tribes, to that point to which we were so anxious to push our way . . . Our animals had laid the ground bare for miles around the camp, and never came towards it but to drink . . . We had to witness the gradual and fearful diminution of the water, on the possession of which our lives depended . . . From its original depth of nine feet, it now scarcely measured two . . . Had the drought continued for a month longer . . . that creek would have been as dry as the desert on either side."

On 13th July it rained. Sturt wrote: "All night it poured down without any intermission, and as morning dawned the ripple of waters in a little gully close to our tents, was a sweeter and more soothing sound than the softest melody I ever heard . . . the moment of our liberation had arrived."

Poole, now confined to a stretcher, was sent back on a dray with some of the men towards Laidley's Ponds (Menindie).

Sturt and the rest of the party headed north, but had travelled only four miles when a rider brought news that Poole was dead. He was buried under a grevillea tree at Depot Glen and the two chastened parties went their separate ways.

In the vicinity of Fort Grey station, scores of jerboas, burrowing ratlike animals with long hind legs, were observed moving about the sandhills. Several were captured, fed on oats and became tame, but eventually they died. Three aboriginal hunters Sturt met had nearly 200 in their bags, which they cooked and ate in one sitting when they camped overnight with the explorers.

A depot camp, surrounded by a low stockade, was established at Fort Grey. Sturt probed due west to check Eyre's claim that the country north of Mt Hopeless was an impassable salt bog, a continuation of the Lake Torrens basin. Sturt encountered Lake Blanche on 5th August, referred to it as Lake Torrens and went back, convinced that Eyre's assessment of the country was correct.

After returning to Fort Grey, Sturt headed north-west, hopeful that he would discover the large mass of water indicated by the migrating birds. As he left, he gave orders that the boat should be painted and made ready for use.

It was not to be. The little party struggled on across Strzelecki and Cooper creeks and into the stony desert that bears Sturt's name. It was now September. Rations were down to five pounds of flour and two ounces of tea a week for each man, plus occasional pigeons and ducks shot by the men.

Passing just west of where Birdsville now stands, the explorers entered sand dune country, the sight of which caused one member of the party to exclaim: "Good heavens, did ever man see such country!" Sturt was now more than 400 miles from Fort Grey and by his own calculations, only 150 miles from the centre of the continent. (The present town of Alice Springs is approximately in the centre of Australia—Sturt was 300 miles from Alice Springs.)

On 8th September, 1845, Sturt turned back to Kuddaree waterhole in the dry sandy bed of Eyre Creek. After trying unsuccessfully to follow up the creek, he retreated to Fort Grey, reaching there on 2nd October. He set out north again on 9th October, with Stuart and two other men, but failed to penetrate as far north as he had already been.

This time Sturt followed up Strzelecki Creek, discovering large permanent waterholes in the bed of Cooper Creek where he crossed it. (Farther downstream, where he had crossed previously, it had been dry.) Pressing on, he crossed the stony desert again, but had to turn back for lack of water only a few miles short of the Diamantina River—where he would almost certainly have found big waterholes. The point at which he retreated, on 21st October, was only a dozen miles from the present town of Birdsville.

Returning to the Cooper, Sturt followed it eastward, meeting numerous very large waterholes shaded by overhanging river gums. Birdlife was prolific, and included pelicans, bitterns and seagulls. Aborigines were present in considerable numbers, living in sizeable domed brush huts, connected by well-trodden paths to each other and the waterholes. Within his first five miles along the Cooper, Sturt counted 71 aborigines.

Two men, one 6 ft 3 in. tall, acted as guides to the party, leading them from camp to camp. At one stage, the guides disappeared ahead over the summit of a hill. Sturt wrote: "We reached the hill soon after the natives had gone over it, and on gaining the summit were hailed with a deafening shout by 300 or 400 natives, who were assembled in the flat below. I do not know, that my desire to see the savage in his wild state, was ever more gratified than on this occasion . . ."

Fortunately, the aborigines were extremely friendly, offering them large coolamons of water, which they calmly held up for the horses to drink from. They also gave the explorers roast duck and small seed cakes and gathered wood for their fire after they had declined an offer to shelter in a newly-built hut. Sturt wrote that the men of the tribe were the finest he had ever seen. When 69 were gathered round him at one time, he wrote that he did not see one who seemed to be less than 5 ft 10 in. tall. The women, on the other hand, were "the same half-starved unhappy looking creatures whose condition I have so often pitied elsewhere".

The tribesmen indicated to Sturt that there was no water to the east, a fact he soon verified by riding out on a vast, arid plain. The horses were beginning to knock up, supplies were running low and Sturt was in poor health. He wrote that he could scarcely climb into his saddle each day.

Naming the watercourse Cooper Creek after the Judge of South Australia, Sturt and his men retraced their tracks to Strzelecki Creek and began the long trek back to Fort Grey. It was now 11th October, 1845.

The depot at Fort Grey was deserted. On Sturt's earlier instructions, the men there had fallen back to Depot Glen when their water supply was almost exhausted and putrid. Sturt and his three companions continued south, rejoining the main party on 17th October.

Another blazing summer was approaching. Creeks and waterholes were rapidly drying out. The party faced another forced sojourn at Depot Glen, which Sturt realized few of them could endure again. If they could reach Laidley's Ponds, they would be safe. There was good water there, plus fresh rations Sturt had ordered when he sent some of his men back from Depot Glen previously. But the only water between the depot and Laidley's Ponds was at Flood's Creek, 118 miles south. If this were dry, the party would perish on its southward dash.

Sturt was ill and unable to walk. Browne and Flood rode south in a cart with 36 gallons of water to see if there was water in the creek. They returned in eight days. Sturt wrote: " 'Well, Browne,' said I, 'what news? Is it to be good or bad?' 'There is still water in the creek,' said he, 'but that is all I can say. What there is is as black as ink, and we must make haste, for in a week it will be gone.' " Sturt continued: "Here then the door was still open —a way to escape still practical . . . but even now we had no time to lose."

Before decamping on that nightmare journey, Sturt records: "The boat was launched upon the creek, which I had vainly hoped would have ploughed the waters of a central sea . . ."

The party struggled back to Menindie, reaching there on 20th December. Fresh supplies and letters from Adelaide were waiting for the explorers. After a few days' rest, Sturt set out for Adelaide, still unable to ride. Reaching Eyre's home at Moorundie on 15th January, Sturt found that his old friend had gone on leave to England.

Sturt concludes his narrative thus: "On the 17th I mounted my horse for the first time since I had been taken ill in November, and had scarcely left Moorundie when I met my good friends Mr. Charles Campbell and Mr. A. Hardy in a carriage to convey me to Adelaide. I reached my home at midnight on the 19th of January, and, on crossing its threshold, raised my wife from the floor on which she had fallen, and heard the carriage of my considerate friends roll rapidly away."

The father of Australian exploration was home from the inland for the last time. There was no inland sea, no fertile land, no prospect of settlement. Only sand and silence and the merciless sun.

Death in the desert, the fate of men and horses in the early days of inland exploration

Sheep grazing on improved pasture in Major Thomas Mitchell's "Australia Felix"

Grazing country along the Hume and Hovell overland route from Lake George to Port Phillip Bay

Strange vegetation of Australia puzzled the explorers. Grass trees like these were found from the cold eastern highlands to the blazing Gibson Desert

The coming of the explorers and the settlers who followed them spelt doom for the original inhabitants of Australia

The unknown north

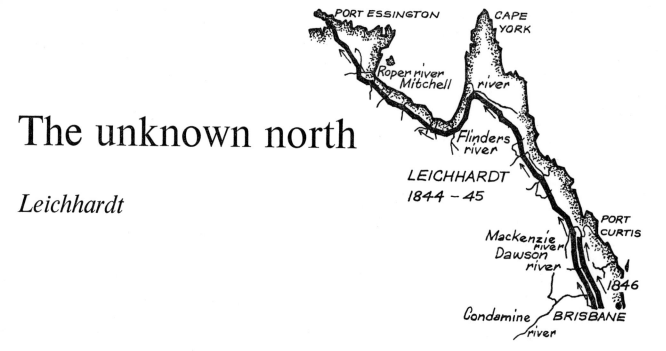

Leichhardt

While Sturt was battling his way south to the Murray in 1845, his old rival, Major Mitchell, was on his way north through Queensland, hopeful of reaching the Gulf of Carpentaria. At the same time, the strangest, most ill-assorted exploring cavalcade ever to brave the Australian wilds was also on its way north.

Led by an eccentric German who affected a Malay coolie hat and a sword, this extraordinary expedition was following its leader's "guiding star" from Moreton Bay to Port Essington, 100 miles north-east of what is now Darwin. Their equipment, or lack of it, was laughable, their supplies were hopelessly inadequate. No one in the party had much idea of navigating; the only bushman, Pemberton Hodgson, resigned in disgust after a few weeks and so did the cook, an American negro.

By some miracle, certainly more by good luck than good management, the party eventually meandered its way across the top of the continent and arrived at Port Essington. Ludwig Leichhardt's faith in his guiding star was apparently justified. The colony acclaimed him.

Seasoned bushmen and all those who knew the gangling Leichhardt fell back in astonishment.

This impossible man had achieved the impossible. How had he done it?

The explorer and writer, Ernest Favenc, in his book on Australian exploration, published in 1888, wrote of Leichhardt: "His Journal reads like the fable of the Babes in the Woods . . . His great confidence in himself led him to ignore or undervalue the fact, patent to others, that he was no bushman either by instinct or training. And he seemed to prefer for companions men like himself, who could not detect this failing . . ."

Favenc is mostly right on this point. Three of his companions were young men aged 15, 19 and 24, fresh out from England. Another was a convict, a former London solicitor, with no knowledge of the Australian bush. Leichhardt had been in the country little more than two years, most of which time he had spent in Sydney. John Gilbert, the naturalist, who joined the party at the eleventh hour, knew something of the Australian bush. His diaries, discovered in the 1930s by Australian naturalist Alec Chisholm, disclosed that he had formed a very poor opinion of Leichhardt, as a man, as an explorer and as a scientist.

How did Leichhardt manage his great feat?

He did, after all, accomplish a colossal journey

of some 3,000 miles, through unknown country, staying out 14 months with supplies that were scarcely sufficient for six months.

The answer is clear to anyone who reads his journal. In addition to the inexperienced new-chums Leichhardt chose to accompany him, were two other men whose names invariably appear last on any list of the members of the exploring party. They were Charley Fisher and Harry Brown, aboriginal guides to the party. Their names should appear at the head of the list of personnel. Without any shadow of doubt, they took Leichhardt and his party to Port Essington. Leichhardt was perhaps their guiding star, indicating the general direction he wanted to travel (for they never would have bothered to make such a journey on their own initiative), but if it were not for the general incentive he provided, Leichhardt might as well have stayed in Sydney. He was, in fact, a general hindrance. He got lost regularly when he went out alone, frequently stampeded the party's horses and cattle when he went among them at night or lost his temper with them while they were being loaded —and mismanaged almost everything.

He had, however, at least one redeeming feature: he knew the value of his "blackfellows". They recovered the stock when they were lost, found water, game and edible plants and alerted the party to the approach of hostile tribes. Realizing this, Leichhardt took any amount of "cheek" from them, even to the point of having some of his teeth punched out by Charley!

When the party's meagre supplies of flour, sugar and tea ran out, Charley and Harry kept the larder full with ducks, kangaroos, emus, flying foxes and other game for the final six months of the journey. Leichhardt was afraid of guns and never fired a shot. Only toward the end of the trip did any of his youthful white companions manage to bag anything for the pot.

No one in the party knew how to handle bullocks and horses. The standard method of catching a horse seemed to be by grabbing it by the tail! Several of the party were severely kicked. The stock were never watched adequately at night; they invariably strayed. Only Charley and Harry were competent to track them and bring them back, sometimes as far as 12 miles.

Without their two "blackfellows", Leichhardt and his men would have lost their horses and bullocks before they were off settled country. Without

Charley and Harry, Leichhardt and his men would have been hopelessly lost within a month of leaving the last station (near the present town of Roma). And they would have starved after eight months in the "wilderness" when their stores ran out.

These facts emerge clearly from Leichhardt's journal, though he glosses them over with his own effervescing self-confidence. To give him his due, he seems not to have *consciously* realized his dependence on his "blacks".

Leichhardt has been criticized for "straying" too far north on Cape York Peninsula before veering west for the goal, Port Essington. But his journal explains the reason for his circuitous route. The party never left water for more than a day. They simply followed across the east flowing streams from their starting point to the latitude of Cairns, where they finally struck a west-flowing tributary of the Mitchell River.

In typical aboriginal fashion (Leichhardt was, after all, more or less in the hands of Charley and Harry), the party simply followed the river course, where the tucker in the form of wildfowl was plentiful. For the two aborigines, the whole journey was obviously a merry, extended walkabout or hunting holiday, with white fellahs to carry the flour, tea and sugar and to supply them with ammunition. Apart from tracking the horses and bullocks which were lost almost daily, they did little work in the camp. On most days, after delivering the stock, they just disappeared into the bush with their guns, to hunt whatever was available. Often they did not reappear until late in the afternoon, after a jolly day of hunting, cooking and feasting. Leichhardt frequently complained about this, but took no action.

On several occasions, Leichhardt tried to reconnoitre westward for water, but as he neglected to carry either food or fluid with him on these sallies, they were necessarily restricted to one day. After getting lost a few times in the early stages, he always took Charley or Harry with him. On the one or two occasions when they were caught out overnight, he writes that his guides complained bitterly about the lack of both food and water.

A study of Leichhardt's own maps shows that he never strayed more than ten miles from water. Taking this practice into consideration, it is obvious that the route he took was the only one open to him. Other explorers frequently travelled over dry stages of 100 miles, but they carried water kegs with them. Leichhardt's party carried only a single two-gallon pot, plus the men's individual drinking quartpots! The well-watered nature of the country through which Leichhardt passed can be judged by the fact that they resorted to using the two-gallon pot for the first time at what is now the Northern Territory border 11 months after setting out.

Having met with the Mitchell River, Leichhardt continued to follow it north-west, though he apparently knew this was taking him considerably out of his way. Only when a more westerly flowing stream was discovered just two miles from the river did he leave it.

After that, by heading south, Leichhardt found he could cut freshwater creeks every 10 miles or so. This made everybody happy—Leichhardt and his European followers because they were headed in the right direction, and Charley and Harry because every day brought them to a new stream and good hunting.

And so the party continued their journey all the way to Port Essington. They survived largely because of Charley's and Harry's prowess as hunters and foragers of native food. Aided by this bush tucker, Leichhardt was able to eke out his beef on the hoof over the whole journey. He started with 16 bullocks and arrived at Port Essington with one, named Redmond.

Although the two aborigines were largely responsible for the success of the expedition, Leichhardt's contacts with the bush aborigines were unsatisfactory and ended in death for John Gilbert, the naturalist. The explorer's habit of having guns fired when aborigines were around probably antagonized them. He also had a habit of stealing food and nets from their camps when the aborigines fled in surprise at his arrival. (In the early stages, he left trinkets in exchange for the items he took, but the aborigines probably didn't understand or appreciate this gesture. Later, he seems not to have bothered about making a "fair exchange".)

Leichhardt's journal reveals that he had a poor opinion of the aborigines. He was, however, a keen observer of their food-gathering methods. He learned perhaps more than any other explorer how to live off the land in the manner of its native inhabitants. He was more than willing to try anything he saw the aborigines eating, no matter how unusual or repulsive it seemed to European tastes. Blossoms, fruits, seeds, nuts, roots, snakes, flying foxes, dingoes, pandanus palms, were all grist to Leichhardt's mill, plus the usual bush tucker of kangaroos, emus and various wildfowl. If other explorers had shown a similar enthusiasm and willingness to experiment, they might have survived instead of perishing.

Charley and Harry were not without fault. The attack on the party which resulted in the death of John Gilbert was almost certainly a reprisal raid following a clash between Charley and Harry and the local tribes. The diaries of Phillips the convict and John Calvert, another member of the party, both suggested that Charley and Harry had molested aboriginal women while absent from the camp, allegedly hunting.

Returning by ship from Port Essington to Sydney, Leichhardt was acclaimed throughout the colony. His critics were confounded. He had taken twice the expected time, but had nevertheless achieved his goal.

Flushed with success, Leichhardt quickly organized another expedition, announcing that he would this time travel from Moreton Bay across the continent to the west coast and then south to Perth!

The journals of John Gilbert, William Phillips, John Calvert, J. H. Mann and Daniel Bunce confirm that Leichhardt was hopeless as a bushman, had few qualities of leadership, could not navigate and was wildly eccentric.

The expedition set out from the Darling Downs inland from Moreton Bay in December 1846. It was a much grander cavalcade than the previous one, comprising seven Europeans, two aborigines (one of whom was Harry Brown), 15 horses, 13 mules, 40 bullocks, 180 sheep and 270 goats. Leichhardt kept no journal, but two of the party, surveyor John F. Mann and Daniel Bunce, botanist, kept diaries. These documents indicate that the expedition was a fiasco almost from the first day.

The stock strayed continually. At one point there was a delay of 25 days while they were remustered after a stampede caused by Leichhardt who had gone among them to "tame" them. When the party reached the Mackenzie River, inland from Rockhampton, the men became ill with fever. Leichhardt's "medical chest" turned out to contain mainly soap, plus a knife and a bullet mould. For weeks the men languished in a nightmare hospital camp, nursing each other as best they could. At one point, Leichhardt announced that he was dying.

The botanist, Daniel Bunce, planted mustard and cress seed to provide fresh greens for the men. On the day he went to harvest his crop, he found Leichhardt had gone down earlier, cut and eaten everything himself! Mann, the surveyor, found Leichhardt stealing sugar and tapioca.

After struggling on another 70 miles, the men rebelled and the expedition returned to the settled areas and disbanded. Leichhardt had apparently made a mistake in taking experienced bushmen and other specialists into his party. They recognized that his incompetence and eccentricities could be fatal to such an expedition.

What were the complaints about Leichhardt? Apart from those mentioned, Bunce and Mann detailed some of their causes for complaint: Leichhardt persistently stampeded the mules and bullocks through outbursts of temper or irrational behaviour. Often, when the animals were being quietly herded together, he would endeavour to speed up proceedings by rushing at them, shouting and waving a stick. Another odd Leichhardt manoeuvre was to suddenly begin beating a pack animal about the head, causing it to rear up and spill its load, sending the rest of the animals off in disarray. On the few occasions that Leichhardt walked at the head of the pack string, he would lead them straight into bogs, stepping aside himself at the last moment without making any attempt to halt the animals.

Leichhardt had the quaint habit of catching horses and mules by the tail. John Mann wrote: "He would persist in trying his taming qualities with the mules; in spite of all cautions, he would walk up to the heels of a mule as readily as to its head; the consequence was that he received such a kick in the stomach from one of them as to completely double him up for some time."

When taxed with cutting and eating Bunce's salad greens, which were intended for the men too sick to move from their beds, Leichhardt retorted: "Let those who want it, gather for themselves." When caught stealing sugar, Leichhardt announced that it did him good! Mann wrote: "On replying that it might do us good, too, he said 'No, it will turn acid in your stomachs.'"

When a bullock was killed for meat, Leichhardt insisted on butchering it with his sword, with the result that a lot of the meat was wasted. On another occasion, he took a duck from the pot and split it with his sword. Taking half for himself, he offered the remaining half to be shared among eight men!

Of Leichhhardt's bushmanship, Mann wrote: ". . . the doctor being the only bad bushman among them—scarcely venturing to trust himself alone out of sight of the camps." A veteran stockman, Stuart Russell, who had a property near Leichhardt's starting point, wrote: "It's my belief that if Dr. Leichhardt do it at all, 'twill be more by good luck than management. Why, sir, he hasn't got the knack of some of us" (for bushmanship).

Speaking of Leichhardt's qualities as a navigator, the Queensland government geologist said it was impossible to prepare an accurate map of the explorer's Port Essington journey from his journal and sketches. "That way madness lies," he wrote. John Gilbert recorded that the first time Leichhardt checked his position by astronomical observations, the party discovered they were only 100 miles from the sea, near Rockhampton, when they had thought they were 340 miles inland! When he took his second observation on 26th June, 1845, near the 16th meridian of latitude, he calculated his longitude at 141 degrees 25 minutes—which placed the party about 20 miles out to sea in the Gulf of Carpentaria!

Such were the navigations of the man who proposed to lead an expedition overland to Perth, across 3,500 miles of uncharted, largely waterless

Ludwig Leichhardt

country. Having taken Leichhardt's measure in the early stages of the journey, his men very wisely decided to turn back.

Incensed at the eight-month debacle which had greatly tarnished his public image, Leichhardt organized a third party to attempt the colossal overland journey to Perth. This time he fell back on his earlier practice of choosing for his companions men with qualifications no better than his own.

Historian-explorer Ernest Favenc wrote in 1888: "Very little is known of the members that composed it; the only thing certain is that it was not at all adapted for the work that lay before it . . ." The Reverend W. W. B. Clarke declared: "The parties that accompanied Leichhardt were perhaps little capable of shifting for themselves in case of any accident to their leader. The second in command (Adolf Classen), a brother-in-law of Leichhardt, came from Germany to join him before starting, and he told me, when I asked him what his qualifications for the journey were, that he had been at sea and had suffered shipwrecks, and was therefore well able to endure hardship. I do not know what his other qualifications were."

Arthur Hentig, a German "gentleman" was another member of the party. The other two Europeans, Kelly and Stewart, were hired as "labourers". Stewart was an ex-convict. These two men have sometimes been described as "bushmen" but this appears to be mere assumption. In view of Leichhardt's previous unhappy experience with bushmen, it is more than probable that Kelly and Stewart were not of the bush.

The two aborigines with the party were Wommai and Billy. Wommai had been on the second expedition, with Harry, the veteran of the first journey. After the fiasco of the second trip, Harry apparently decided his luck was running out and disappeared.

The ill-fated party set out from Roma in April, 1848, on their proposed two-year journey. They had what Ernest Favenc described as "utterly inadequate" rations and equipment. (Leichhardt took with him only 800 pounds of flour, to last six men for two years; Augustus Gregory, on one of his journeys in search of Leichhardt, packed 1,000 pounds of flour to last eight men five months, plus such items as 400 pounds of bacon, 300 pounds of sugar, 600 pounds of meat biscuit, 600 pounds of dried and fresh meat.) In addition to his flour, Leichhardt seems to have taken only "some sugar and salt", plus 120 pounds of tea. He had written in his Port Essington journal that he found tea a most beneficial drink, without sugar.

There are conflicting figures on the number of animals Leichhardt took with him on his last journey. Probably he had about 12 horses, 12 mules, 50 bullocks and possibly some goats.

After they left Roma, none of the men or animals was ever seen again. The interior swallowed them up—but not as mysteriously as is generally supposed.

Augustus Gregory, sent to search for Leichhardt in 1855, discovered a Leichhardt camp on Elsey Creek in 1856. Gregory's party had landed from a ship near the mouth of the Victoria River in the Kimberleys. His journal entry for 13th July, 1856 reads: ". . . proceeded down the creek (the Elsey) . . . several trees cut with iron axes were noted . . . There was also the remains of a hut and the ashes of a large fire, indicating that there had been a party encamped there for several weeks; several trees from six to eight inches in diameter had been cut down with iron axes in fair condition and the hut built by cutting notches in standing trees and resting a large pole therein for a ridge . . . Search was made for marked trees but none found, nor were there any fragments of iron, leather, or other material of the equipment of an exploring party, or of any bones of animals other than those common to Australia. Had an exploring party been destroyed here, there would most likely have been some indications, and it may therefore be inferred that the party had proceeded on its journey. It could not have been a camp of Leichhardt's in 1845, as it is 100 miles southwest of his route to Port Essington, and it was only six or seven years old, judging by the growth of the trees; having subsequently seen some of Leichhardt's camps on the Burdekin, Mackenzie and Barcoo rivers, a great similarity was observed in regard to the mode of building the hut, and its relative position in regard to the fire and water supply, and the position in regard to the great features of the country was exactly where a party going westward would first receive a check from the waterless tableland between the Roper and Victoria rivers, and would probably camp and reconnoitre ahead before attempting to cross to the north-west coast. This creek is named Elsey Creek on the map."

This find by Gregory is almost unassailable. No other explorer had been in the area before 1856 except Leichhardt. The only possible error seems to be that it could have been one of Leichhardt's 1845-6 camps. For this to be so, Leichhardt's map would need to be wrong by 100 miles—quite possible in his case. But his detailed description of the country does not fit the Elsey terrain, nor is there any mention in his journal of a lengthy camp being made on the one spot in October 1845 (the period when he was travelling along the Roper about 90 miles from Elsey Creek).

The camp was almost certainly Leichhardt's and almost definitely not one of his 1845 camps. It must therefore have been a camp made on his journey which commenced in 1848.

Gregory (and later Favenc) formed the opinion that after leaving Roma and striking the Barcoo, Leichhardt had recoiled from the dry western country and headed north as he had done twice previously.

After reaching the Mackenzie River he would have followed his old route across the Gulf country to the Roper, this time veering west for the Victoria River, instead of north for Port Essington. By following the Roper upstream, he would have come to Elsey Creek.

This theory fits in perfectly with Leichhardt's previous mode of never pushing more than a dozen or so miles beyond known water. He almost certainly was not equipped to carry a large quantity of water, had no experience or record of travelling in dry country and probably headed north-east, not west, from the Barcoo. Stories of "Leichhardt trees" (marked "L") in the Cooper country and in the Simpson Desert can be discounted. Ludwig Leichhardt needed to camp on water every night, and in country well stocked with wildfowl and edible plants for the pot. There is no "Leichhardt country" west of the Barcoo.

So the Leichhardt mystery begins not in western Queensland but west of Elsey Creek in the Northern Territory. Apparently creeks and waterholes were scarce at this stage and the explorer established a base camp on the Elsey while he and his men scouted ahead for a likely route. He probably tried following the Elsey upstream until it became a series of waterholes eventually petering out in dry country west of Daly Waters.

It was apparently not the monsoon time when he arrived at Elsey Creek, because there would have been plenty of water available and no need for a

76

base camp. Perhaps he waited for the summer rains and then made his way across to the tributaries of the Victoria River. Or he could have proceeded north-west from Elsey to the Katherine River system, downstream into the Daly River country and south to the Victoria system, eventually striking the Kimberleys.

But this is conjecture. The last probably correct known fact about Leichhardt is that he established a base camp for some weeks or months on Elsey Creek, not far from the present settlement of Mataranka. The key to the Leichhardt mystery after that lies with him in his unknown, lonely grave.

Leichhardt's route from the Roma district along the eastern slopes of the ranges to the Burdekin River near Charters Towers traverses what is now some of Queensland's finest cattle grazing country. The coast between Townsville and Cairns is a popular tourist resort and sugarcane growing area. On the rich Atherton Tableland, tobacco is one of a variety of upland crops.

Across the peninsula to the Gulf of Carpentaria there are few roads and the beef cattle grazing lands are largely unimproved and sparsely fenced. From Normanton, through Burketown and Borroloola to the Roper River, Leichhardt's route is as difficult as it was in the explorer's time. Only bush tracks, impassable in wet weather, connect the isolated cattle stations and missions of the lagoon country. Sealed "beef" roads link Borroloola with the Barkly and Stuart highways. Mining developments on the Macarthur River may give these roads added importance.

Arnhem Land and most of the adjoining country through which Leichhardt passed remain superficially the same as it was in the explorer's time. But mining on Gove Peninsula and other places, plus large-scale, American-financed agricultural and grazing developments seem destined to bring great changes to the land first penetrated by our comic opera explorer.

The first camel

Late in July, 1846, a small, ill-fated exploring party set out from Adelaide, bound for Western Australia. Called "The Northern Exploring Party", it numbered five white men, one aborigine, six horses, two carts, 13 goats and one camel.

John Ainsworth Horrocks led the group, and among his companions was the famous landscape painter, S. T. Gill.

After eight weeks in the field, Horrocks accidentally shot himself when the trigger of his musket fouled some harnessware. Seriously wounded,

he continued to write his journal as his party nursed him homeward. He died on 1st September, 1846, soon after reaching an outlying station.

His brief and tragic expedition had achieved nothing, but it is remembered because it was the first to use a camel for exploration in Australia. The animal had been the only survivor among a number of camels brought by ship to Adelaide. The original importer, disappointed over the loss of his animals, apparently sold the one remaining camel to Horrocks.

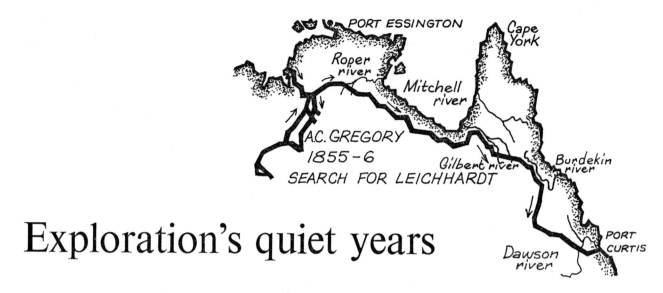

Map labels: PORT ESSINGTON, Cape York, Roper river, Mitchell river, A.C. GREGORY 1855-6, Gilbert river, Burdekin river, SEARCH FOR LEICHHARDT, Dawson river, PORT CURTIS

Exploration's quiet years

Gregory and others

While Leichhardt was on his way home by ship from Port Essington late in 1845, Major Mitchell was setting out from Sydney, bound for the Gulf of Carpentaria. As usual, he was at the head of a small army, heavily armed and fully provisioned. Edmund Kennedy, later to become an explorer in his own right, and to die tragically on Cape York Peninsula, was Mitchell's second in command.

The party included 30 men, eight drays, three carts, two boats, 80 bullocks, 17 horses and 250 sheep. After striking the Darling, Mitchell and his army plodded slowly upstream, eventually heading slightly west of north to strike first the Warrego and then the Barcoo rivers. Although it tended south-west for the 100 miles he traced it, Mitchell decided that the Barcoo eventually veered north and flowed into the Gulf of Carpentaria. He named it the Victoria River.

Mitchell did not care to test his theory. Instead, he retraced his steps and then went north to follow the Belyando River almost to its junction with the Burdekin.

His course was roughly parallel to that of Leichhardt's, but 175 miles farther inland. Had he continued a little farther, Mitchell would have crossed Leichhardt's recent tracks on the Burdekin.

Having reached a point no farther north than Mackay, the major lost interest in trying to reach the Gulf and returned home.

Although he made some useful discoveries of good grazing land beyond the Maranoa and on the Warrego, Mitchell's efforts were somewhat overlooked in a colony with eyes only for Ludwig Leichhardt, who by then had returned to Sydney to marshal his second expedition.

Sturt arrived back in Adelaide in January, 1846, and was for a while the hero of the colony. But his discoveries of useless desert lands were quickly eclipsed by the fanfare of publicity associated with Leichhardt's triumphant return to Sydney late in March. His news was all good: fine, well-watered grazing country all the way to the Gulf. There was land for everyone in the north!

The old rivals, Sturt and Mitchell, smarted in the shadow of a new star—and a "foreigner" at that!

In the same year, 1846, the Gregory brothers were probing inland from the west coast. Augustus Churchman Gregory, then assistant surveyor in

Charley Fisher and Harry Brown, the aboriginal guides responsible for the success of Leichhardt's 1845 journey to Port Essington

Travellers with sheep and cattle on the Darling River. Explorers usually travelled with stock, to provide a supply of fresh meat

John McDouall Stuart country, between Coober Pedy and Lake Eyre

Milparinka, not far from Sturt's old camp at Depot Glen, is almost a ghost town. Gold brought it brief prosperity

The road north to Alice Springs parallels Stuart's route across the continent

the colony of Western Australia, led the party. His brothers Frank and H. C. Gregory accompanied him. Frank was second in command. The brothers had four horses and provisions for seven weeks.

They set out from Perth on 7th August, 1846, and headed north-west, circumnavigating the great dry saltbed known as Lake Moore. Their journey took them 200 miles inland, where the country became harsh and inhospitable. At one dry stage, they dug 20 holes near a dry lake in search of water. Poisonous gastrolobium was a hazard for their horses. A seam of coal was discovered on the Irwin River, about 300 miles north of Perth.

The party returned to Perth on 21st September, having made a round trip of 953 miles in six weeks. No major discoveries of useful grazing land were made. All the indications were that the interior of the vast colony was arid desert. The hopes of the Perth settlers were dashed.

In the next two years, the brothers made several short journeys of exploration from likely places along the coast. They travelled to their starting points by ship and were usually ashore with their horses for only a few days.

By 1848, all the known pastoral country round Perth was fully stocked and newly arrived settlers were anxious to take up new country. The surveyor-general, Captain John Septimus Roe, led an expedition overland to Albany and then headed for the interior.

Keeping about 100 miles inland, he followed the line of the coast to a point between the present towns of Norseman and Esperance. The country proved unattractive, and so Captain Roe wheeled south toward the coast and returned to Albany. From there he travelled almost directly across to Busselton, discovering considerable areas of useful grazing country on the way. He returned over his 1830 route along the coast via Bunbury to Perth.

While Roe was still in the field, Augustus Gregory was instructed by the colonial secretary to explore the country north of Perth as far as the Gascoyne River. His orders were specific: he was to keep approximately 100 miles inland as far as the Gascoyne, then follow it to its mouth and return home along the coast. Gregory was also cautioned against unnecessary conflict with the aborigines, in a letter from R. R. Madden, the colonial secretary: ". . . you must be well aware it is no less impolitic than cruel to come into actual collision, wantonly, unadvisedly, and maliciously, with the natives; and, on the contrary, that it is no less human than politic to leave no angry recollections of white people, where the footsteps of travellers . . . must be expected to follow yours."

Enmeshed for some time in red tape, Gregory finally set out in September, 1848. As he pushed north, the summer sun burned with increasing intensity, drying up the land around him. Lack of water forced Gregory to turn back soon after crossing the Murchison River, well short of the Gascoyne, which was over 100 miles farther north. Apart from this setback, the expedition was generally successful. Large tracts of good land were discovered in the Geraldton district on Champion Bay, and south as far as the Irwin River.

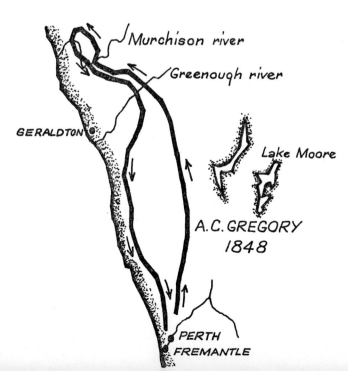

Gregory reported: ". . . I trust that our attempts to render the expedition serviceable to the colony have not proved unsuccessful, especially as the result has been the discovery of several fine portions of good grassy land near Champion Bay, which . . . will render available a tract of pasturage sufficiently extensive to relieve the present overstocked districts; the estimated quantity of land suitable for depasturing sheep being about 225,000 acres, exclusive of 100,000 acres on the Irwin, the greater portion of which, however, is better suited to agricultural purposes . . ."

Gregory was sent off again to Champion Bay on 1st December, 1848, at the height of the summer, to show Governor Fitzgerald his discoveries, particularly a vein of lead he had noted in the bed of the Murchison River.

The trip lasted only 10 days and ended in something of a debacle. Some angry tribesmen approached the party. Notwithstanding the advice offered so recently to Gregory by the colonial secretary on the need to avoid collision with the natives, the Governor immediately shot one man dead. This precipitated a running battle, in which the Governor received a spear through his thigh, delivered "with such force as to cause it to protrude two feet on the other side, which was so far fortunate, as it enabled me to break off the barb and withdraw the shaft", Gregory reported.

Fighting their way back to the coast, the party scrambled back on board the ship in Champion Bay on 11th December and sailed for home.

On the other side of the continent, Edmund Besley Kennedy had been sent in 1847 to check his previous commander Major Mitchell's unlikely theory that the "Victoria River" flowed into the Gulf of Carpentaria. Kennedy followed the stream south-west to the point where Sturt had turned back in 1845. Mitchell's "river" was only a tributary of Cooper Creek, discovered and named by his old rival Sturt! Kennedy renamed the stream the Barcoo River.

Apart from this rather negative discovery, Kennedy found nothing new and his expedition aroused little interest.

But Kennedy was destined to achieve lasting fame the following year, in tragic circumstances. He set out in 1848 on the most disastrous expedition to that date in the annals of Australian exploration. His starting point was Rockingham Bay, near the present township of Tully. He was bound

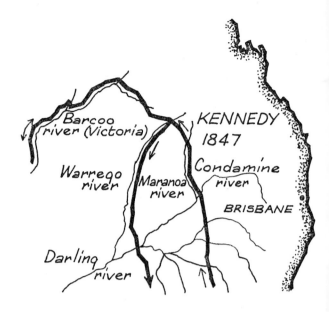

for the northern tip of Cape York Peninsula, where it was hoped to establish a port for trade with the islands off south-east Asia (the "East Indies" of the period).

The trip was a disaster from start to finish. The place chosen for the landing was completely unsuitable. The bay was too shallow for the expedition ship, the barque *Tam O'Shanter*, to get closer than a quarter of a mile from shore. The horses had to swim this distance to the mainland. One drowned. Once ashore, the party was hemmed in by almost impenetrable tropical jungle and found itself on the wrong side of a large river. Before they could escape from Rockingham Bay, the party had to ford the river by converting their carts into temporary boats with the aid of tarpaulins.

Kennedy had 12 companions, including one

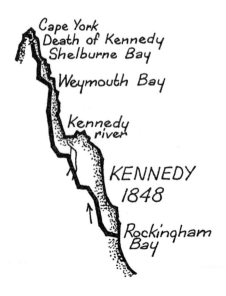

aborigine, named Jacky, destined to be the hero of the expedition. The cavalcade proved far too large and heavily equipped for the wet and boggy jungle country it tried to penetrate. There were 28 horses, three carts, 100 sheep, a canvas sheepfold, 24 pack saddles, nine sets of harness, 40 hobble chains and straps, 28 tether ropes, each 21 yards long, firearms, powder and shot, tents and other camp equipment, plus a generous amount of supplies, including one ton of flour, 600 pounds of sugar, and 90 pounds of tea. After finally getting everything ashore between 21st and 24th May, the party didn't get away from Rockingham Bay until 6th June.

On 4th July, when some aborigines assumed a threatening attitude, Kennedy ordered his men to fire on them. Four were either killed or seriously wounded. This was perhaps a mistake, because the party was harassed for the rest of the journey by hostile tribesmen. On 15th July the carts and some of the heavier equipment were abandoned in rough jungle country.

On 14th August, Kennedy discovered that the cook and some of his men had been stealing food. Supplies were much lower than expected. Tribesmen attacked the party on 10th and 15th September. On the 16th, Kennedy found that food pilfering was still going on. By 2nd October, supplies were getting dangerously low. A horse was killed on that day and not even the blood was wasted—it was mixed with flour to make a grisly damper.

Tribesmen attacked again on 10th October. The horses and sheep were weak and dying. When shot, they provided little sustenance. By 22nd October, three men were seriously ill and the party was in low spirits.

On 11th November the last sheep was killed. There were only nine of the original 28 horses left. On the 13th, at Weymouth Bay, Kennedy split his party, leaving eight of his men while he pushed on quickly to meet H.M.S. *Bramble*, waiting at Port Albany on the tip of Cape York.

It was now more than five months since the party had left Rockingham Bay. They had battled their way north for 500 miles—a daily average of three miles.

Kennedy and his four companions took with them 18 pounds of flour and all the remaining dried meat (75 pounds), leaving two emaciated horses and 28 pounds of flour for the eight men remaining at Weymouth Bay.

Botanist William Carron was left in charge of this party. His diary records that six of the men died between 16th November and 28th December. There was heavy rain and the meat from the horses they killed soon turned putrid. Aborigines surrounded the camp almost continuously, waiting a chance to attack. Sometimes they brought the men scraps of old fish, but Carron with justification mistrusted their motives. He described several times how tribesmen tried to sneak on them with spears while others were offering them pieces of "almost rotten" turtle. On another occasion, two unarmed men approached ". . . and endeavoured to persuade one of us to go across a small dry creek, for a fish which another of the rascals was holding up to tempt us. They tried various methods to draw our attention from the rest, who were drawing their spears along the ground, with their feet, closing gradually around us, and running from tree to tree, to hide their spears behind them. Others lay on their backs on the long grass, and were working their way towards us, unnoticed, as they supposed . . ."

Meanwhile, Kennedy struck trouble soon after leaving Weymouth Bay when one of his men accidentally shot himself. Leaving two men with the wounded man at Shelburne Bay, he made a frantic dash for Port Albany, accompanied only by Jacky. They had almost 100 miles to go.

Torrential rain fell. Kennedy was weak from hunger and unable to proceed except on horseback. Jacky urged him to abandon the horse because it left "too much track" for the local aborigines to follow. Eventually they were attacked when only a few days' travel out of Port Albany. Kennedy was hit a number of times and killed. Jacky escaped and after eluding his attackers for several days, emerged on shore at Port Albany and signalled to the waiting ship, the *Ariel*. It was 23rd December, 1848.

On learning that Kennedy was dead and that three dying men waited at Shelburne Bay and another eight survivors might be still alive at Weymouth Bay, Captain Dobson set sail as soon as possible, on 24th December. Jacky guided the ship to Shelburne Bay, but when a party went ashore, they were unable to find the camp where the three men had been left.

At Weymouth Bay, Captain Dobson and his men found only two survivors of the eight-man party: botanist William Carron and a man named

Goddard. Dr Adoniah Vallack, of the *Ariel*, described the scene: "On the other side of the hill, not 200 yards from us, were two men sitting down, looking towards us, the tent and fire immediately behind them; and on coming up to them, two of the most pitiable creatures imaginable were sitting down. "One had sufficient strength to get up; the other appeared to me like a man in the very last stage of consumption . . . Carron's legs were dreadfully swollen, about three times their natural size."

Carron later wrote: "I was reduced almost to a skeleton. The elbow bone of my right arm was through the skin, as also the bone of my right hip . . ."

In April, 1849, Jacky guided a party from the brig *Freak* to the site of Kennedy's murder, but was unable to find the shallow grave in which he said he had buried the explorer. Various items of equipment were recovered, including Kennedy's journal and maps, which Jacky had concealed in a hollow tree. Unfortunately they had been badly damaged by the heavy monsoon rains.

At Shelburne Bay, Jacky led a shore party in search of the camping site of the three abandoned men. Only a few remnants of their stay were found, including a leather pistol holster.

Thus ended the disastrous expedition to Cape York by Edmund Kennedy—a tragic, ill-conceived journey that had accomplished nothing.

The basic error of this expedition seems to have been in making no provision for the party to return to Rockingham Bay if the country became impassable. Judging from the only available journal of the trip, that of William Carron, the spirit of exploration had left the party within the first month and they would have returned to their starting point if arrangements had been made for a ship to call there. Instead, the journey in its earliest stages became a struggle for survival, with the party's only hope being to somehow battle through almost impossible conditions to reach the waiting ship at Port Albany.

The continual harassment by the aborigines could not have been foreseen, but the onset of the monsoon season was predictable. Arrangements should have been made for other coastal rendezvous points, in case the journey took longer than expected—as it did.

The performance and calibre of the aborigine Jacky deserves special note. He was unstintingly praised by William Carron, Captain Dobson and Dr Vallack of the *Ariel*, Captain Simpson and Chief Officer Macnate of the *Freak* and Captain Elliot of the *Harbinger* (the ship accompanying the *Freak*). Their findings fully substantiated Jacky's story and their reports indicated a high regard for the man they obviously considered to be the mainstay of the entire expedition.

Early in 1852, the first search was made for Leichhardt, now officially deemed to be missing. It was headed by Hovenden Hely, who had been with Leichhardt on his brief, ill-fated second expedition. Aborigines had brought in rumours of a massacre of white men out in the Warrego country west of Roma. Hely found two camps on the Maranoa he thought were Leichhardt's, because of some trees marked with something like an L-shape. Although he found no other evidence, Hely returned, convinced Leichhardt must have perished in central Queensland. The trees were possibly at some of Kennedy's 1847 camps.

On his great overland trek from the Victoria River near the Kimberleys to Rockhampton, Augustus Gregory made an energetic search for Leichhardt. Most of his journey was along the fringe of the well-watered coastal country favoured by Leichhardt. Wherever a watercourse led inland, he followed it, in case Leichhardt had done the same.

He followed Sturt Creek south-west into the interior for some 300 miles. This took him south of the present site of Billiluna homestead and Balgo Mission, to the usually dry Lake Gregory.

Assuming Leichhardt did manage to travel overland from his camp on Elsey Creek to the headwaters of the Kimberley systems, Sturt Creek offered him the only apparent direct route toward Perth. But Gregory found no trace of Leichhardt along Sturt Creek. The German would more likely have followed his usual practice of sticking close to the coastal streams. This would have taken him into the Kimberleys toward Derby near the mouth of the great Fitzroy River.

There is no possibility that Leichhardt could have pushed south west from the Fitzroy. He would have needed to cross 400 miles of the Great Sandy Desert to his next water on the De Grey River—a task quite beyond him, considering his record and the probable state of his party by then.

If Leichhardt reached the Kimberleys, he almost certainly died there, probably at the hands of the independent, warlike tribesmen of the area.

Monsoon rains would quickly wash out any traces of the expedition.

After exploring Sturt Creek, Gregory returned briefly to the Victoria River and set out for Moreton Bay in April, 1856. After finding the old Elsey camp, he proceeded to more or less duplicate Leichhardt's 1845-46 route, accomplishing the journey in only 10 months without drama or mishap. Leichhardt had taken 14 months and had staggered into Port Essington empty-handed and in tatters, more as a survivor than as a successful explorer.

Gregory led another expedition in search of Leichhardt in 1858, starting from the Roma district in Queensland. He found an authentic Leichhardt camp on the Barcoo near the present town of Blackall. Dry country to the north and west prevented him searching farther for traces of Leichhardt. He wrote he was "compelled to abandon the principal object of the expedition", and followed the Barcoo and Cooper south-west. From his journal, it is clear that Gregory regarded this trip as a journey of exploration, rather than a search. He had, after all, found clear evidence two years earlier that Leichhardt had reached Elsey Creek—and the German could hardly have reached that point by travelling down the Barcoo and Cooper Creek toward Lake Eyre!

However, Gregory obviously welcomed the opportunity to lead a well equipped expedition into the interior and acquitted himself well, as usual. Travelling via Strzelecki Creek and Mt Hopeless, he reached Adelaide in five months. In this he would have been aided by Sturt's maps of 1845, showing the trend of Strzelecki Creek toward Mt Hopeless.

Apart from the tree marked with an "L" on the upper Barcoo, no further trace of the Leichhardt expedition was found.

Augustus Gregory had once again accomplished a long journey of exploration through the unknown, arid country that had stopped earlier travellers. He was perhaps the most accomplished of all Australian explorers. Through meticulous planning and careful reconnoitring of the route ahead, he never got into serious trouble—and therefore never made the headlines or captured the public imagination as did the fatal blunderers, Leichhardt and Burke.

Apart from his many journeys, Augustus Gregory served the cause of exploration in other ways.

A. C. GREGORY 1858 SEARCH FOR LEICHHARDT

He was a gifted mechanical improviser and developed the modern Australian pack-saddle from the cumbersome, inconvenient English "sumpter horse furniture" that had been used previously. He also invented a new compass, known as Gregory's Patent, which Ernest Giles later described as "unequalled for steering on horseback, and through dense scrubs where the ordinary compass would be almost useless . . . steering on camels in dense scrubs, on a given bearing, without a Gregory, would be next to impossible".

Meanwhile, Frank Gregory was busy on the west coast, establishing a reputation as an explorer in his own right. In 1857, after travelling by ship to Gantheaume Bay, he followed up the Murchison River for several hundred miles. In 1858, good rains made it possible for him to push overland from the upper Murchison to the Gascoyne River, which had been the goal of the Augustus Gregory expedition in 1848.

Near Mt Augusta, Frank Gregory noted: "We here met with strong evidences of the cannibalism of the natives; at a recently occupied encampment we found several of the bones of a full-grown native that had been cooked, the teeth marks on the edges of a bladebone bearing conclusive evidence as to the purpose to which it had been applied; some of the ribs were lying by the huts with a portion of the meat still on them."

At this point, Gregory gave his longitude as 111

degrees, which placed him about 100 miles out to sea, between Carnarvon and North-West Cape. He was in fact near 117 degrees.

In 1861, Frank Gregory landed at Nickol Bay, near the present iron port of Dampier, to look for land suitable for growing cotton. The American civil war had caused a shortage of raw cotton for the cotton mills established in Britain during the Industrial Revolution.

Gregory spent six months examining the country between the Fortescue and De Grey rivers, penetrating inland to the Hamersley Range, which he named. He noted that magnetic rocks made his compass useless in some areas. His report stated that he found between two and three million acres suitable for colonization, including 200,000 acres suitable for cotton on the deltas of the De Grey and other rivers.

There had not been an exploring expedition to arouse the enthusiasm of all the colonies since Sturt's and Leichhardt's epic journeys of 1845. Even Augustus Gregory's monumental treks sparked off little comment—because they had been accomplished efficiently, without drama, and had failed to open the way to any rich new country. The Kennedy tragedy aroused the sympathy of all colonists, but nothing more.

The nation waited for some inspired hero to tear open the heart of the continent and reveal the hoped-for Promised Land of milk and honey, preferably around an inland sea.

There was a ripple of excitement in Perth when Frank Gregory returned, but few settlers rushed to colonize this arid country—which remains almost uninhabited to this day, outside the recently established mining towns. Frank Gregory's efforts passed almost unnoticed in the eastern colonies.

The state of the colonies—1850-60

Public interest was wrenched away from exploration at the beginning of this tumultuous decade by the cry of "Gold!" Discoveries were made in 1851 at Bathurst in New South Wales and at Bendigo, Castlemaine and Ballarat in Victoria. (Gold had been reported several times in the Bathurst district, by a number of people, beginning with Strzelecki, but the news had been successfully suppressed. One story goes that Governor Gipps, on being shown a gold nugget by the Reverend W. B. Clarke, said: "Put it away, Mr. Clarke, or we'll all have our throats cut!")

The New South Wales and Victoria gold rushes brought new colonists into Australia at a fantastic rate. In a single month in Melbourne in 1852, nearly 20,000 diggers arrived. Between 1851-57, 400,000 immigrants came to Australia.

Everyone was off to the diggings. The colonies of New South Wales and Victoria were in an uproar. Business for a time came to a standstill.

Farms were deserted. The brief, tragic mutiny at Eureka Stockade near Ballarat in December 1854 was the news story of the decade. Then public fears grew concerning the number of Chinese diggers arriving in the colonies. By 1857, there were 40,000 of them in Victoria. The cry of "Yellow peril!" went up. Riots broke out and legislation was introduced to stop the Asian flood.

Squatters, small farmers and business men who at first were almost ruined by the gold rushes, eventually made fortunes from the diggers. Prices soared as demand rose for every type of produce. Teamsters charged up to £150 a ton to transport goods to the diggings. Successful diggers seeking to buy land found prices had sky-rocketed from £2-10-0 to over £50 an acre.

In this unprecedented, rip-roaring decade, exploration to the far interior of the continent faded from the public mind.

88

The great south to north race

Burke and Wills, Stuart

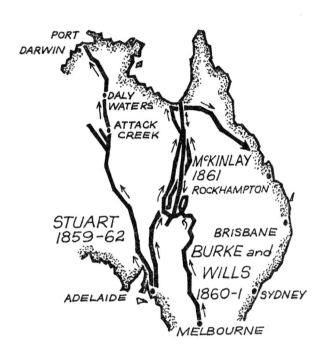

In the 1850s, Australia's only means of communication with England and the rest of the world was by sailing ship. After 1859, news travelled somewhat faster, coming by a telegraphic landline to India, from where despatches were sent on by ship. By 1860, plans were made for a submarine cable to link the Australian colonies direct with London, by way of India. Opinion was divided on what route the cable should follow. Western Australia hoped it would come to that colony. New South Wales thought the cable should touch the mainland on the northern coast on the Gulf of Carpentaria, and come overland to Sydney. South Australia suggested the cable should be brought to a point on the northern coast near the Victoria River and south across the continent to Adelaide.

To hasten discovery of a practical overland route for the proposed telegraph line, the South Australian Government offered a prize of £2,000 for the first expedition across the continent from south to north. The offer fired the public imagination across the continent.

Captain Charles Sturt's companion and surveyor on his 1845 expedition, John McDouall Stuart, was the first man to try. After settling in South Australia, he had made a number of journeys of exploration in the Coober Pedy area and to Lake Eyre (then thought to be the northern reaches of Lake Torrens).

Stuart had been financed by various pastoralists and business men, including William Finke and James Chambers. His discoveries of pastoral country and mineral bearing country amply repaid his backers.

He set out to cross the continent from a station near Strangways, east of Lake Eyre South, on 2nd March, 1860. He had two companions and 13 horses.

A few months later, a much larger, heavily equipped cavalcade set out from Melbourne, also

ROEBOURNE
Nickol
Bay

ONSLOW
Hamersley range
Ashburton river

De Grey river

1861
Fortescue river

F. T. GREGORY
1857 - 58 - 61

Gascoyne river

1858

Murchison
river

1857

Gantheaume
Bay

See: *Exploration's quiet years*

The Burke and Wills expedition setting out from Melbourne in 1860. This was the first use of camels on a major journey of exploration

Survivor John King, living with aborigines, welcomes the relief expedition led by Alfred Howitt. Both paintings by S. T. Gill, from the originals in the Dixson Galleries, Sydney

Typical sand country of the interior, photographed in the Mallee District of Victoria

The famous DIG tree on Cooper Creek, a lonely monument to the ill-fated Burke and Wills expedition

Stark ranges in the Glen Helen area, west of Alice Springs. Gosse saw this country in 1873

Lake Eyre rarely contains water. Like most inland lakes, it is usually hard salt. Mirages tricked some explorers

The strange convolutions of the Macdonnell Range in central Australia. McDouall Stuart first saw these lands

Desert oaks west of Ayers Rock. Gosse and Giles explored this kind of country in 1873

bound for the north coast. It was led by Robert O'Hara Burke, a policeman, no more qualified as an explorer than Ludwig Leichhardt. He was to meet a similar fate.

The expedition was organized by a committee of the Royal Society of Victoria, headed by Sir William Stawell. Public subscription raised £6,000 and the Government supplied a similar amount, making a total of £12,000. Camels were imported from India, good horses were found, equipment was lavish and stores abundant, no expense was spared. Why a totally inexperienced, hot-headed policeman was chosen to head the expedition remains one of the greatest mysteries of Australian exploration.

While all Melbourne cheered, the impressive cavalcade set out on 19th August, 1860. There were 15 Europeans, three Indians, 25 camels, plus 22 riding and cart horses and 21 tons of stores and equipment, sufficient for one year. By the time the party reached the farthest outpost of civilization at Menindie, eight weeks later, Burke had quarrelled with most of his party and six men withdrew, including his second in command, George Landells.

At Menindie, which consisted of a rough bush pub, a few shacks and a river-boat landing stage, Burke hired what replacements he could. One man was Charles Gray, a former sailor, then working at the pub. Another was William Wright, a local station manager, whom Burke chose to appoint as his second in command.

There had been good rains to the north. The country was green and the creeks were flowing. For reasons that are not clear, Burke split his party and headed off with some of his men, 16 camels and 15 horses, guided by Wright, who knew the country well. At a point near the present town of Tibooburra, Burke sent Wright back to bring up the rest of the party to Cooper Creek, where he intended to establish a base camp.

Wright, it seems, was anxious to learn whether his appointment to the expedition, casually made by Burke in the Menindie pub, had been confirmed in writing by the committee of the Royal Society in Melbourne.

At Wright's insistence, Burke had sent a letter off to Melbourne from Menindie soon after the oral arrangement was made. Wright, a cautious bushman, knew little of Burke and understandably did not want to risk perhaps a year, perhaps even

his life, only to find out later that he was not officially recognized as a member of the party.

When he returned to Menindie, there was no letter of confirmation and some of the expedition party refused to take orders from him. His suspicions were further aroused when some of Burke's cheques given to the publican for supplies were returned marked "not sufficient funds". (This came about through official red tape and the inertia of the committee.) Wright sent a letter off with a horseman, asking the committee for its decision on his appointment, plus the £250 Burke had asked for in his earlier communications to Melbourne.

This all took time—several months. When the committee realized that half the expedition was stalled at Menindie waiting on its decision, it quickly confirmed Wright's appointment and sent an additional £400. Reassured, Wright prepared to set out when a constable named Lyons and a companion arrived on horseback with an urgent message for Burke. It came from the head of the committee, Sir William Stawell, advising Burke that his rival Stuart had just returned to Adelaide, having failed to cross the continent. There was no longer any need for Burke to hurry or take undue risks. (Stuart had reached Tennant Creek, where he had discovered some gold, but had been turned back, sick with scurvy and desperately short of supplies, by warlike aborigines who had skirmished with him at a place he named Attack Creek.)

Wright might or might not have offered to take the message on to Burke; but constable Lyons seems to have insisted on delivering the message himself and commandeered a number of Wright's horses in order to proceed post haste. This caused Wright further delay while he scouted round the district for suitable replacement mounts.

Time passed and the country that had been green and well-watered turned dry and brown.

Wright eventually got away from Menindie on 26th January, 1861, having received the committee's letter of confirmation a fortnight earlier. Plagued by lack of water and feed, his cavalcade faced the same problems as almost destroyed Sturt in the area in 1845. But Wright pushed on, discovering on the way Constable Lyons and his companions starving beside their dead horses. They had failed to deliver their message.

By the time Wright and his party reached permanent water on the Bulloo River, 70 miles short

E

of the Cooper, three of his man were dead and the others sick with scurvy. Wright suggested to the medical officer, Thomas Beckler, that the sick men should be sent down to Menindie.

Beckler refused to allow this, saying the men were unfit to travel the distance over such bad country. Wright then suggested the party should move on the remaining 70 miles to Cooper Creek, but Dr Beckler rejected this suggestion also. So the party sat down on the Bulloo with a mountain of supplies and did nothing. Part of their stores consisted of dried carrots, turnips and other preserved vegetables specially included to prevent scurvy. Dr Beckler apparently had no faith in these and never used them. At a subsequent enquiry into the failure of the expedition, he defended his strange action by claiming he did not have time to prepare the vegetables, saying: "They were quite hard and require dissolving or being kept in water for some time . . ."

Meanwhile, what of the impatient explorer Burke?

He had reached Cooper Creek safely, set up a base camp and after waiting five weeks for Wright, again split his troops and hurried north. Leaving William Brahe and three others at the depot camp, Burke set out with William John Wills, John King, Charles Gray, one horse and six camels. They had stores for three months.

It was now 16th December, the height of summer. But the party was again lucky in its timing. Rains had fallen previously, bringing up good grass and filling the creeks.

Although they suffered some hardships and difficulties, caused largely by boggy country, the explorers had a comparatively easy 750-mile walk along the 140th meridian of longitude to the Gulf. They reached a tidal mangrove swamp near the mouth of the Flinders River on 11th February, 1861. Mud and mangroves prevented them from catching a glimpse of the open waters of the Gulf.

Supplies were low, but could have been easily replenished, according to King, by shooting some of the teeming wildfowl of the area. Burke was in a hurry to return, and so the party began an urgent march after only one day of rest. Rain poured down. The country was a quagmire. Gray complained of being ill, but was ignored.

The party marched on, night and day. Wills in a letter to his father wrote: ". . . our forced marches prevented our supplying the deficiency (food) from external sources", confirming King's statement regarding the available wildfowl. A slower pace might have enabled the party to maintain good physical condition. They had six camels and one horse to eat, plenty of game, plenty of water, plus flour, sugar, tea and dried meat sufficient for five weeks. (They had taken eight weeks to travel from Cooper Creek to the Gulf.)

But Robert O'Hara Burke was in the sort of frantic hurry a man would be in if he had told William Brahe at the depot camp not to wait longer than 12 weeks. Brahe later told the inquiry that Burke had said to him: "If we are not back in three months, consider us dead." Brahe in fact waited four months before abandoning the depot camp. Knowing Burke's character, this is just the sort of impetuous statement he could have made to Brahe. Why else would he be in such an unseemly hurry to get back to Cooper Creek, when the season was good and he had ample hard stores and meat on the hoof?

It was not until more than five weeks had passed and all the stores were used that Burke finally paused long enough to kill a camel, on 30th March. Most of the meat must have been left behind, because only 10 days later, Burke's horse was shot and cut up to dry. A week later, on 17th April, Gray died.

Three days later, at 7.30 p.m. on 21st April, the party staggered in to the depot camp on Cooper Creek to find it deserted. Brahe and his men had left only nine hours earlier, leaving a buried cache of 50 pounds of flour, 60 pounds of sugar, 60 pounds of oatmeal, 20 pounds of rice and 15 pounds of dried meat.

The bitterness of this moment for the three men can scarcely be imagined. Burke seems to have been completely crushed by it and any vestige of common sense evaporated. He formed a wild plan to follow Augustus Gregory's route down Strzelecki Creek to Mt Hopeless.

Wills and King suggested they should follow Brahe's tracks, but they were over-ruled. So the ill-fated trio struggled downstream, physically and spiritually weak. Their camels bogged and died or strayed off. The aborigines tried to befriend the party, offering them cakes of nardoo seeds, fish and edible plants.

The explorers accepted some of this, but Burke was suspicious of the aborigines and several times chased them away, sometimes firing shots over their heads.

While the ill-fated trio were starving a few miles downstream, Brahe and Wright came up from their Bulloo River camp to see if their leader had returned. It was a very brief visit. They stayed only 15 minutes at the now famous "DIG" tree, saw nothing disturbed and returned. (After digging up the stores, Burke and his companions had carefully filled in the hole, leaving a message inside, but in their misery and panic had omitted to carve a message on the tree.)

Burke, Wills and King wandered aimlessly up and down Cooper Creek, living chiefly on food from the aborigines and a few crows and other birds King shot. Much of their time was spent pounding nardoo seeds into flour, which they made into cakes. Wills died on 26th June. Burke died a few days later.

Left to his own devices King soon fell in with the aborigines and was kindly treated by them. His statement shows how wrong Burke (and Wills) were in mistrusting the motives of the people of the Cooper. They showed King the compassion so notably lacking among the European settlers of the period toward the aborigines. These were the tribes later shot down like animals at the time when Sir Thomas Elder took over their country for grazing.

On 15th September, King was rescued by the relief expedition under the command of Alfred William Howitt. Later, King was feted as the first man to cross Australia from south to north and live.

A public inquiry into the disastrous expedition was held in Melbourne, and William Wright was greatly criticized. But his tardiness was largely the result of the slowness of the Melbourne committee in confirming his appointment, aggravated by commandeering by Lyons of some of his horses. Dry conditions similar to those that marooned Sturt in 1845 slowed his progress northward.

The crux of the matter was Brahe's abandonment of the depot at Cooper Creek. Wright's failure to arrive no doubt worried Brahe, but he was not short of supplies when he left. According to his statement, he stayed on a month longer than he was required to under Burke's instructions.

In retrospect, it seems that the bulk of the blame for the disaster must lie on Burke's shoulders, with the Melbourne committee, Wright and Brahe as contributors to the failure, in that order.

Once it was realized in Melbourne that O'Hara Burke's expedition was in trouble, a relief party led by Alfred William Howitt was despatched to render assistance. Howitt left Melbourne in June, 1861 and met Brahe's returning party on the Loddon River near Castlemaine. After telegraphing the alarming news to Melbourne, Howitt sped on to Cooper Creek to look for possible survivors.

Bushman-explorer William Landsborough was sent by ship from Melbourne to the Albert River on the Gulf of Carpentaria, with instructions to reconnoitre south for Burke's party. Ex-policeman Frederick Walker set out overland from Rockhampton to rendezvous with the Landsborough expedition supply ships on the Albert River. (In 1865, Walker blazed the route for a telegraph line from Cardwell to the Norman River on the Gulf. The Queensland Government hoped the submarine telegraph cable from India would meet the Australian mainland at this point. The Cardwell-Norman River telegraph line was built in 1870-1, but was never linked with the cable from India.)

After various mishaps, the two ships *Victoria* and *Firefly* put Landsborough ashore on 16th November, 1861, and waited for his return.

When news of the disaster reached Adelaide, Scottish-born squatter John McKinlay was chosen to lead a relief expedition to follow Gregory's old track along Strzelecki Creek to the Cooper and beyond. He left Adelaide on 16th August, 1861, taking with him nine men, 26 horses, four camels, 12 bullocks and 100 sheep.

On 15th September, Howitt's party discovered John King living among the aborigines at Cooper Creek. The man who found him was Edwin Welch, second in command of the relief party. He reported that as he approached a group of tribesmen, they withdrew, "leaving one solitary figure apparently covered with some scarecrow rags and part of a hat, prominently alone on the sand. Before I could pull up, I had passed it, and as I passed, it tottered, threw up its hands in the attitude of prayer, and fell on the sand." It was John King.

After burying the remains of Burke and Wills, Howitt and his party lingered a few days while King regained enough strength to travel. Then, after rewarding the aborigines for their kindness to King, Howitt set off back to Melbourne.

A month later, John McKinlay's party reached Cooper Creek from the South Australian side of the border. On 21st October, an aborigine guided him to a place about 50 miles north of the Cooper, where he said white men had been killed and buried by some tribesmen. McKinlay dug out a shallow grave and found a skeleton, completely bare of flesh, dressed in a flannel shirt with short sleeves, the skull marked by what he judged to be two sabre cuts and bearing only a trace of decomposed hair.

Near by, McKinlay noted a considerable quantity of "the dung of camels and horse or horses, evidently tied up a long time ago". The implication of his remark seems to be that he assumed a camp had been made here for some time, certainly more than one night. Further investigation revealed a second grave, "evidently dug with a spade or shovel, and a lot of human hair of two colours, that had become decomposed . . . In and about the last grave named, a piece of light blue tweed, and fragments of paper and small pieces of a Nautical Almanac were found, and an exploded 'Eley's cartridge' . . . also . . . a tin canteen . . ."

News reached McKinlay while he was still at Cooper Creek that Howitt's party had found King alive, and the remains of Burke and Wills. This caused McKinlay to puzzle over the graves he had found, at the spot he now assumed to be where Burke, Wills and King had buried the unfortunate Charles Gray. Only six months had passed since Gray's death, yet the body had become a completely clean skeleton. In a hot, dry climate where bodies tend to mummify, this seemed unusual to McKinlay. He wrote: ". . . the body I found was perfectly decomposed, and on the skull, even, there was not a particle of skin, but as bare as if it had lain in a grave for years."

Nor could he understand why there were two graves instead of one.

Eventually he assumed that Burke's party must have been attacked by aborigines at the camp where Gray died and that the explorers had buried an aborigine shot in the struggle. McKinlay wrote: "I am still under the impression that when Burke's diary is published it will show of some affray with the natives about this place . . ." It did not. Nor did Wills's journal or survivor John King's statement say anything of a multiple burial. Further, a map drawn from information derived from Wills's journal places Gray's grave almost due west of the Cooper Creek depot. McKinlay's map shows the two graves he found at a point well to the northwest of the depot.

In view of these discrepancies, it seems highly probable that the graves discovered by McKinlay had nothing to do with the Burke and Wills expedition. Therefore, the grave of Charles Gray has never been discovered. Who were the two Europeans buried in the graves discovered by McKinlay? This may remain a mystery forever.

Having learned the fate of Burke and Wills, McKinlay decided to press on northward to the Gulf of Carpentaria. The season, following the rains that had dogged Burke and Wills, was good. Feed and water were plentiful in most places. McKinlay and his men reached the Gulf on 19th May, 1862, becoming the second exploration party to cross the continent from south to north. He was the first man to overland sheep across the continent. The journey had taken nine months.

Landsborough had meanwhile travelled 200 miles south-west of the depot ships on the Albert River to discover and name the Barkly Tableland. But he found no trace of Burke and Wills. Then Frederick Walker's party arrived from Rockhampton, saying they had crossed the missing explorers' tracks along the Flinders River, east of the Albert. This was in December, 1861. After re-stocking, Walker returned to the north Queensland coast and made his way home to Rockhampton. Landsborough set off to the south-east, arriving almost 15 weeks later at a station on the Warrego River in central Queensland.

When McKinlay reached the Gulf, the depot ships, and Frederick Walker and William Landsborough had departed. Near the coast, McKinlay found some trees marked by Landsborough some three months earlier, in February, 1862. His supplies were now running low and he and some of his men were suffering from recurring sickness. The party set out for Port Denison, now Bowen, on the Queensland coast. The 700-mile walk became a nightmare in the later stages. Close to starvation, the explorers reached a station on the Bowen River early in August, 1862. They had left Adelaide in August, 1861.

Meanwhile, John McDouall Stuart made several further attempts to cross the continent. In November, 1860, leading a South Australian Government expedition, he had set out a second time from Adelaide. This time he went another 100 miles north of Attack Creek, his previous farthest point, just north of Tennant Creek. Then rough scrub and lack of supplies forced him to retreat. Stuart reached Adelaide in September, 1861, on board the steamer *Lubra*, which he had joined at Port Augusta.

The Government and his two private backers, Chambers and Finke, showed their continuing faith in Stuart by immediately backing him for another journey. An advance party set out late in October. Stuart joined the expedition at Moolooloo station in late December. The full cavalcade left the farthest out station on Chambers Creek on 2nd January, 1862.

Although officially told to make for the Victoria River once beyond the point he had reached previously, Stuart had decided to make for the Adelaide River. He made this decision upon receipt of a letter from Lieutenant Frank Helpman, who had been aboard the H.M.S. *Beagle* during the survey of the north-west coast. Helpman pointed out that the mouth of the Adelaide River seemed an ideal site for a port, whereas the Victoria was unsuitable for shipping.

After much casting about for water in the vicinity of Newcastle Waters, Stuart's party made their way via Daly Waters to the Roper River, crossing Augustus Gregory's 1856 tracks not far from Elsey Creek. Veering north-west, they reached the headwaters of what Stuart thought was the Adelaide River and followed it down. This was in fact the Mary River.

Difficult country in the last stages of their journey forced them away from the river to the east. The coast was reached on 24th July, 1862. The place where Stuart first saw the sea is now called Point Stuart, on the eastern tip of Chambers Bay.

After one effort to make west along the coast to the mouth of the river (which he still thought was the Adelaide), Stuart began his monumental and almost fatal 2,000-mile homeward journey.

Stuart was a sick man by the time the party regained the Roper River. He had spent the major portion of the past five years on exploratory journeys in harsh country, living and working hard on short rations. Scurvy now assailed him and he became an invalid, scarcely able to stay in his saddle.

Fortunately, most of Stuart's companions were younger, fitter men, well able to care for their leader and shoulder his burdens on the homeward trek. In the later stages of the journey, Stuart was carried on a litter between two horses for a distance of 400 miles. His second and third officers, Kekwick and Thring, nursed him as best they

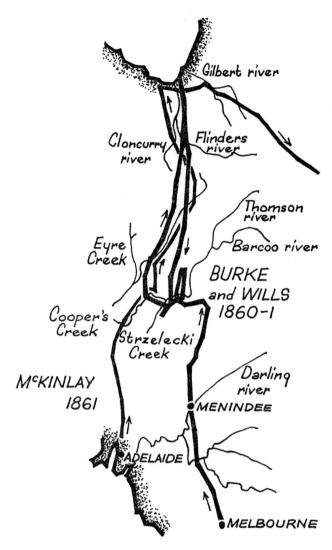

could, feeding him flour and water gruel when he was unable to eat solid foods. At times Stuart lost his power of speech, his eyesight failed periodically and he vomited mucus and blood.

Four months after leaving Point Stuart, the returning party reached the northernmost station in South Australia at Mount Margaret. Stuart rested here a few days and had another spell at Moolooloo station, farther south. At Kapunda he boarded a train, arriving in Adelaide on 17th December. Doctors immediately ordered him to bed for a fortnight.

On 21st January, the remainder of Stuart's cavalcade reached Adelaide and there was a triumphant procession through the town. Bands played, mounted police and cavalry turned out and crowds cheered as Stuart (accompanied by John McKinlay) led his little cavalcade down King William street to the treasury buildings, where the Governor, Sir Dominick Daly and Lady Daly waited to receive him. Later there was a banquet lasting into the small hours, at which 14 toasts were raised to the new hero of Australian exploration, John McDouall Stuart.

In April, Stuart received his prize of £2,000, which he immediately turned over to friends to invest for him. He was too ill to take any interest in financial matters. Stuart's invested prize money yielded him a return of only £150 a year, which was insufficient to maintain him in his invalid state.

After several lean years, during which his health continued to fail, Stuart sailed home to his family in England, leaving Adelaide in April, 1865. Later that year, the South Australian Government invested a further £1,000 on Stuart's behalf, which brought his total yearly income up to almost £300. (Charles Sturt, who was also living in England at that time, was receiving a pension of £600 yearly from the South Australian Government, in recognition of his explorations.)

Sick and partially blind, Stuart died in England on 4th June, 1866. The first man to cross the continent at its centre, his fame had been brief, his reward small. Although he did not die in an unknown grave, it can be said the harsh Australian inland claimed Stuart just as surely as it did Burke and Wills.

The present-day traveller can approximately duplicate the routes followed by the ill-fated Burke and Wills expedition and by John McDouall Stuart. A reasonable good-weather bush road follows the Darling River between Wentworth and Menindie. A safer and more reliable route is the Silver City Highway, linking Wentworth with Tibooburra, via Broken Hill.

From the Queensland border, the track to Cooper Creek is fair in good weather, but not recommended for novice bush drivers. From Cooper Creek to Betoota and Birdsville, tracks can be negotiated by conventional vehicles in skilled hands, weather provided. North from Birdsville through Bedourie and Boulia to Mt Isa, the road is fair. Burketown, on the Gulf of Carpentaria, can be reached via reasonable roads from Cloncurry or Camooweal, except in the annual wet season.

The New South Wales part of the journey is through eroded sheep country. Most of the Queensland route is through eroded cattle country.

John McDouall Stuart's route is more easily followed, via a rough but well-defined road linking Port Augusta and Alice Springs through a stark, inhospitable eroded landscape. North from Alice Springs the road is bitumen to Darwin, through monotonous scrub country with few scenic attractions until Katherine is reached, on the Katherine River.

The northern frontier

McKinlay

After the short-lived military camps at Port Essington between 1824 and 1849, there was no permanent settlement on Australia's north coast west of Cape York.

In 1863, the British Government empowered South Australia to annex as its "Northern Territory" all the land passed through by McDouall Stuart. This area had previously been part of New South Wales.

In 1864, the South Australian Government sent Boyle Travers Finniss to establish a settlement at Escape Cliffs, near the mouth of the Adelaide River in Port Darwin. South Australia was particularly anxious to open a trade gateway for the colony and also a landing point for the proposed submarine telegraph cable link from India.

As Government Resident, Boyle Finniss did little toward founding a town or port, but merely camped with his 40 men at Escape Cliffs until his party was removed in 1866, on the advice of John McKinlay.

McKinlay was sent up by ship in November 1865 to see what Finniss had accomplished and to explore the surrounding countryside. He found that Finniss had done next to nothing and had not even bothered to bring up all his stores from the beach where he landed. "A greater scene of desolation and waste could not be imagined. As a seaport and a city, this place is worthless," McKinlay reported.

Finniss was recalled and, despite his lack of enterprise at Escape Cliffs, he later became the first Premier of South Australia.

McKinlay's visit was ill-timed, coinciding with the wet season. He set out north-east to rendezvous with a depot ship at the mouth of the Liverpool River. He was accompanied by 14 men with provisions for 10 weeks, plus 35 horses. Rain pelted down incessantly for six weeks. There was plenty of rank grass, but the horses starved on it. Stores were spoiled and several horses died or were lost in the rising swamps.

Eventually, at the Alligator River, McKinlay found himself unable to proceed or retreat. The whole country was a quagmire. His men were on short rations and would soon be starving. The horses were emaciated and dying.

McKinlay, a master of improvisation, decided to build a boat and sail back to Escape Cliffs in Port Darwin. He ordered the remaining 29 horses killed and their hides stretched on a rough framework of bush saplings. This rickety, improvised punt measured 21 feet by 9 feet by 3 feet. The horse-flesh was stored aboard to sustain the 15 men on their journey. A tent was cut up to make a sail. Oars were fashioned from saplings. Water-bags were made from surplus horse skins. Somehow, this incredible craft, named *The Pioneer*, made the 200-mile journey back to Escape Cliffs. Undeterred, McKinlay borrowed a boat and explored the coast westward as far as the Daly River, which he recommended as a port site in preference to the one finally chosen.

McKinlay then returned to Adelaide and after being commended for his work, resumed his life as a squatter on the run he had occupied for some years.

Work on the overland telegraph line started in

August, 1870, and was completed early in 1872. Construction parties totalling 500 men worked from the north and south, setting up 37,000 poles to carry the wires linking Adelaide and Port Darwin. Cost of the job was half a million pounds, an astronomical amount in those days.

In the course of construction, permanent water was found at Alice Springs, only 40 miles off Stuart's route—the discovery made by surveyor W. W. Mills, on 11th March, 1871. A telegraph station was established at Alice Springs and others to the north at Barrow Creek, Tennant Creek, Powell Creek, Daly Waters and Katherine. To the south there were stations at Charlotte Waters, The Peake, Beltana, and other places. There were no automatic repeater stations in those days and each message had to be transmitted by morse operators from one station to the next.

John Ross surveyed the final route of the telegraph line, which for the most part followed fairly closely in Stuart's tracks.

The port of Darwin, despite its growing size and population, remains basically a public service town. For many years dubbed "Australia's northern gateway", it handles chiefly inflowing traffic. For a century the theoretical export centre for a vast hinterland bigger than France and Germany, Darwin remains without any sizeable industries and exports very little.

Visiting ships invariably unload goods and rarely pick up any cargo. Almost everything used in Darwin, from foodstuffs and household items to building materials and machinery, is imported from the southern States. Darwin airport handles an ever-increasing flow of oversea air traffic, including goods and passengers.

Southern tourists flock to Darwin in the winter season, by planes, ships, buses and private cars. There is always a sprinkling of cattlemen, crocodile shooters and other colourful characters in town—but if public servants and tourists disappeared from the streets, Darwin would be almost deserted.

Painting by John Longstaff of Burke, Wills and King at the DIG tree on their return to the deserted depot camp on Cooper Creek

103

Overleaf: The grassy plains of the Kimberleys, locked in by rocky spinifex ridges, were first explored by Alexander Forrest in 1879

John Kennedy dying in the arms of his aboriginal guide Jacky after an attack by tribesmen on Cape York Peninsula

A waterhole on Sturt Creek, near Lake Gregory in northern Western Australia. Augustus
Gregory was first to visit this area, in 1856

Caves east of Lake Gregory contain old aboriginal paintings. Warburton passed south of here
in 1873

In the western country

The Forrest brothers

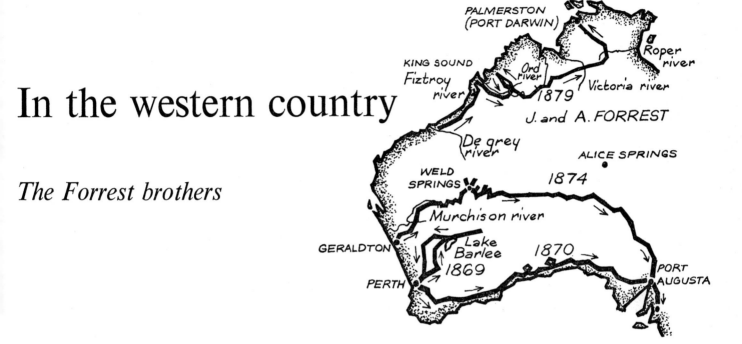

Apart from Hamilton Hume, John and Alexander Forrest were the only major explorers of this continent who were Australian-born. This seeming anomaly may arise from the fact that most early bushmen would not bother pushing into arid country which their local knowledge and experience told them would be dangerous and unrewarding.

Born and bred in the bush around Bunbury in Western Australia, John and Alexander Forrest combined sound, careful bushcraft with a love of adventure to become the first and only Australian-born explorers of the dry inland. They also had luck on their side, for the most part striking good seasons which were denied their exploring contemporaries, Warburton, Gosse and Giles.

John was trained as a surveyor, after the manner of his idol, John Oxley, His first chance at exploring came in 1869, when he was given command of a small Western Australian Government expedition to search for Leichhardt relics. Aborigines had brought in stories of white men murdered far to the north-east of Perth. Forrest set out in April, 1869, with three white and two aboriginal companions. They had six riding and 10 pack horses, plus rations for three months.

Forrest proceeded carefully, never shifting his base camp from one waterhole until all the country ahead had been meticulously examined for more. A single discovery of water rarely satisfied him. He and his two aboriginal companions kept searching, in case a better supply had been overlooked. This policy was to pay off in later expeditions, when Forrest discovered springs and waterholes missed by Gosse and Giles. It also enabled him to stay longer in places where water was scarce, because prior examination of the country enabled him to move his base camp from one small pool or soak to another, while his scouts looked ahead for fresh supplies along the proposed line of travel.

The Leichhardt relics turned out to be the bones of horses abandoned by the explorer Austin some years earlier. Farther east, Forrest discovered Lake Barlee, a vast sticky salt bog in which he almost lost some of his horses. Eventually he rounded the lake and got as far as the present town of Leonora. Here, on 6th July, 1869, Forrest and his small party turned back. They reached Perth a month later, having travelled approximately 2,000 miles on the 113-day expedition.

107

No useful or encouraging discoveries had been made, but Forrest's reputation as a competent and determined explorer was established.

His next job was another government-inspired venture: to find a practical overland route around the Great Australian Bight to Adelaide. Forrest's instructions were to follow Eyre's 1841 route, but to range inland where practical in search of water-holes and pasture.

Arrangements were made for the expedition to rendezvous with a supply ship, the *Adur*, at various points along the coast. This meant that Forrest did not face the same dangers that Eyre did in 1841. He was assured of fresh rations and water every few hundred miles.

Forrest's brother Alexander accompanied him this time, as second in command. A policeman and a farrier were included in the party, and two aborigines—one being Tommy Windich, who had been with Forrest on his previous journey. The party had 15 horses and carried 30 gallons of water, with sufficient rations to get them to their first rendezvous point with the *Adur*.

They set out overland from Perth in March, 1870, bound for Esperance Bay, 450 miles away. Here they waited for the *Adur* to bring in more supplies. Then they moved on to Israelite Bay, 120 miles eastward. Surface water was scarce, but rains had brought up good feed for the horses.

The next rendezvous was at Port Eucla, 400 miles around the Bight, near the South Australian border. Grass was plentiful, but water was just as scarce as it had been in Eyre's time. The only water Forrest could find was that marked on Eyre's map, among sandhills at the end of a long line of perpendicular cliffs. To get it, the explorers had to dig wells 15 feet deep.

Just before leaving the cliff tops and coming down to the sandhills, Forrest and his men passed near the site of Baxter's murder, 29 years earlier. They found no skeleton but, at the sandhills camp, saw the bones of the horse Eyre had slaughtered for meat. Baxter's bones, being lighter than those of a horse, were perhaps carried off by dingoes, or blew away in the wind.

Forrest's journey from Israelite Bay to the sandhills camp took 13 days. Eyre, weak and emaciated and delayed by the murder of Baxter, took 23 days to accomplish the 200-mile stage.

The remaining 170 miles to Eucla occupied Forrest another six days. After meeting the *Adur* in the Bay, Forrest recorded his impressions of the trip so far: "Since leaving Cape Arid I have not seen a gully or watercourse of any description— a distance of 400 miles."

At least there had been good feed all the way for the horses, and drinking water in small rock-holes filled by recent showers. But now Forrest's luck changed and he experienced real hardship and difficulties. There was no feed for his horses and no surface water at all.

The animals had their last drink at Eucla on 13th July and did not get another until 17th July, almost four days later (90 hours, according to Forrest's journal). By this time, he spoke of their being in "a frightful state . . . Some had difficulty keeping up . . . I have never seen horses in such a state before, and I hope never to again. The horses which four days ago seemed strong and in good condition, now appear but skeletons, eyes sunk, nostrils dilated and thoroughly exhausted."

Compare this story, along with Ernest Giles's statement that three days and three nights is near the maximum that horses travelling in such country can go without water, with Eyre's story that his horses *on two occasions went seven days and seven nights without water*.

After rounding the head of the Great Australian Bight on 17th July, the explorers found ample water by digging in the sand dunes. There were no more stony cliffs. At Fowler's Bay the *Adur* was waiting with fresh supplies. Then the party travelled overland direct to Port Augusta. They arrived triumphantly in Adelaide on 27th August, 1870.

Again, Forrest had made no encouraging discoveries, but he had mapped and described much of the country that in a few years was to form the route of the overland telegraph linking Perth with the eastern colonies. His journey also confirmed Eyre's opinion that there was no suitable country for an overland stock route within 30 miles of the coast. All the indications, also, from observation and the stories of local aborigines, were that the country got decidedly worse farther inland.

On 12th July, 1872, Forrest applied to the Governor of Western Australia for assistance to make a journey of exploration from Geraldton to the overland telegraph line, approximately along the 26th parallel of latitude.

Months passed and it became known that Ernest Giles, Colonel Warburton and William Gosse were all in the field, attempting to cross from the overland telegraph line to the west coast and Perth.

The Western Australian authorities asked Forrest to wait and see how his rivals fared. (He had proposed to start his expedition early in 1873. Giles, Warburton and Gosse had all started from Adelaide between July and September, 1872. Giles had pushed west from the telegraph line in August of the same year, but Warburton and Gosse did not leave Alice Springs until April, 1873.)

When it was learned that Giles's first expedition had failed, that Gosse had retreated and that Warburton had arrived starving and sick on the north-west coast, Forrest was given permission and assistance to make his attempt. As things turned out, the delay contributed greatly to his success. If he had set out when he wanted to, Forrest would have been turned back by the same dry season that had stopped Giles and Gosse.

Alexander Forrest was again second in command of the party, which included Tommy Windich, tracker, Tommy Pierre, tracker, James Sweeney, farrier, and James Kennedy, police constable. They had a string of 20 horses. After travelling by ship to Geraldton, on Champion Bay, the explorers turned their faces eastward on 1st April, 1874.

They headed north-east to the Murchison River, which they followed inland to a point near what is now Meekatharra. This area had previously been explored by the Gregory brothers, but on the fifth week, Forrest and his party were in unknown country.

The going proved tough. Approaching the Carnarvon Range north east of Wiluna, Forrest wrote: "I had expected to find a river running to the east, but instead . . . we had not gone many miles before we entered a spinifex desert which lasted without any break worth mentioning for 600 miles."

On 27th May, Tommy Windich found a series of deep waterholes which Forrest delightedly named Windich Springs. "They are the best springs I have ever seen," he wrote. "Pools 12 feet deep and 20 chains long . . ." The explorers shot five ducks and three possums and celebrated the occasion with a feast.

Good rain had fallen some weeks earlier and Forrest wrote that he was "confident for the next 100 miles". About 90 miles to the north-east, they found more good water at a place Forrest named Weld Springs. Emus and pigeons were plentiful and there was ample grazing for the horses. Aborigines had been sighted regularly and, while the explorers were camped at Weld Springs, 50 or 60 warriors attacked them. After several warning shots failed to turn the aborigines back, Forrest reluctantly shot one man and the "battle" ended. The attack had been made on 13th June.

Next day, Forrest and his companions built a stone hut, 10 feet long, nine feet wide and seven feet high, as a protection against further attack. From this base the explorers ranged eastward, but could find no sizeable waterholes. Rock holes that would hold water after rain were dry.

Before leaving Perth, Forrest had received a copy of Gosse's recently completed map. He knew from this that he was only 250 miles from known water—but the distance was too great for his horses. Weeks of scouting passed. Alexander Forrest discovered a small soak and the party moved camp a few miles eastward.

The expedition was on the verge of retreating westward to Weld Springs when rain was observed falling well to the east. On 8th August, Tommy Windich and John Forrest rode out some 30 miles and found that previously dry rock holes were now full. Elated, the party broke camp and headed eastward.

On 10th August, Windich pointed out a tree marked with an axe. Next day, horse dung and tracks were seen on the ground. This puzzled Forrest, who knew from his map they could not be signs of the Gosse expedition. He wrote: "We are not in the latitude of Mr. Gosse by 15 miles . . . I cannot account for this. The tracks may be Mr. Giles's." They were. Later on, Forrest came to the place where Giles had taken "gnow's" (lowan) eggs from a mound.

Near this point, Forrest's party discovered Barlee Springs, missed by Gosse and Giles, who had both searched for water in the area. Another 60 miles brought them to Giles's Fort Mueller, where they discovered a tree marked "E Giles—Oct. 7, 73".

From this point, the party had a comparatively easy journey to the telegraph line, following Gosse's tracks most of the way. They arrived in Adelaide on 3rd November, 1874, where a crowd of 20,000 greeted them.

It was another first for the Forrest brothers and Tommy Windich. But once again, they brought no good tidings. Out in the loneliest part of the continent ever visited by man there was only silence, spinifex and sand.

Alexander Forrest had better luck in 1879, when he led an expedition of his own to the Kimberleys and then overland to the telegraph line at Katherine. (Alexander McRae had briefly explored the Fitzroy river district in 1866.)

He reported 25 *million* acres of good pastoral country, a grossly over-optimistic assessment. Largely as a result of Forrest's extremely favourable reports, much of the Kimberley country was taken up by the MacDonald and Durack families in the middle 1880s.

His expedition started from the town of Roebourne on 29th February, 1879. Forrest had four white companions, two aborigines and 26 horses. They followed the coast to Roebuck Bay, the present site of Broome, where they met three pearling luggers up from Perth.

Good previous rains made their coastal trip along the edge of the Great Sandy Desert easy. Their worst hazard was the large grey mosquito of the north-west coast.

Travelling north-east of Broome, Forrest struck the great Fitzroy River on 8th May and followed it upstream. He travelled overland for a brief visit to Collier Bay and returned to trace the Fitzroy's east branch for another 100 miles. Leaving the Fitzroy, he crossed the Ord River in June and spent some time examining the area. The country was lush after the recent wet season and Forrest was understandably impressed with the luxuriant growth of native grasses.

Farther on, he reached the Victoria River. After more survey work, he pushed on to the Katherine telegraph station, reaching there on 29th September, 1879.

Apart from reporting huge areas of rich grazing country, Forrest described the aborigines of the area as friendly. He suggested they would give little trouble to intending settlers of the district—another prediction that proved wrong.

Although his journey covered a considerable distance through unknown country, Alexander Forrest's success came about in some measure through luck. A dry season would have stopped him long before Roebuck Bay. If he had visited the Kimberleys in the dry winter season, his report of the country would have been less optimistic but more accurate.

In August, 1968, I followed Colonel Peter Warburton's route from Alice Springs northwest to Lake Gregory on Sturt Creek. From here the scarcely discernible Canning stock route heads west to Godfrey's tank near Mt Cornish, then south into the Great Sandy Desert. At this point, the Colonel persisted due west, a foolish decision considering the sad state of his party. The Fitzroy River and comparatively safe country in the Kimberleys was only ten days' march due north.

It was very nearly a fatal mistake on the part of Warburton—and I considered I would have been equally foolish to hazard the journey in a single vehicle, almost a century later. This spinifex and sand country remains as dangerous today as it was in 1873. No grazing empires have been established there. Only an occasional temporary oil search track penetrates its sandy, waterless wastes.

Until oil or other riches are discovered beneath its surface, the Great Sandy Desert is likely to remain a magnificent, silent desolation.

110

The colonel goes west

Warburton

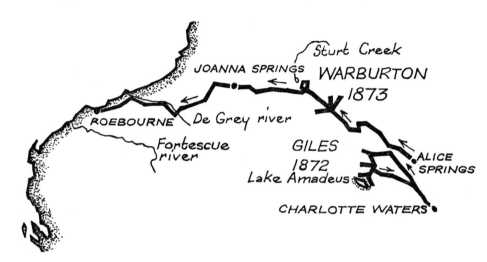

The overland telegraph line provided a series of bases for exploratory journeys westward into the interior of Western Australia. This was now the largest remaining tract of unexplored territory on the continent.

There was no longer much hope of finding an inland sea. All the evidence obtained on the earlier journeyings of the Gregory and Forrest brothers indicated arid land, probably desert. But the lure of the unknown was sufficient to inspire several men to vie with each other for the honour of being first to cross from the overland telegraph line to the west coast.

The three contenders for the title were Colonel Peter Egerton Warburton, William Christie Gosse and Ernest Giles.

Giles was first off the mark, getting into the field from the Peake telegraph station with two companions, 15 horses and a dog in August, 1872. He was financially backed by the Danish-born Victorian Government botanist, Baron Ferdinand von Mueller. On this trip Giles discovered Palm Valley on the Finke near Hermannsburg Mission.

Farther out, he was blocked by the Ehrenburg Mountains and later by Lake Amadeus, beyond which he could see a mountain he named Mount Olga. Giles fell out with his two companions and they all returned to the telegraph line and parted company.

Making his way south alone, Giles heard from some aborigines that Gosse had passed through to the north recently. This was on 22nd November, 1872. A few days later, at Charlotte Waters telegraph station, Giles met Warburton, also on his way north. Backed by Sir Thomas Elder and Sir Walter Hughes, who supplied him with 17 camels and two Afghan drivers, Warburton had left Adelaide on 21st September, 1872.

No doubt greatly chagrined to know his rivals were in the field, Giles continued south, busily planning a second expedition with stauncher, more amenable companions.

Gosse's expedition, though it started west of Alice Springs, finished up south of Giles's route and got as far as the Western Australian border, near the present-day boundary corner of South Australia and the Northern Territory. Gosse inadvertently dodged Lake Amadeus and discovered and named Ayers Rock.

Meanwhile, Colonel Peter Egerton Warburton,

111

accompanied by his son Richard Egerton, surveyor J. W. Lewis, a European cook, an aborigine named Charlie and two Afghans, probed northwest from Alice Springs. Warburton, aged 60, was a rather stiff-necked former Indian army officer and a retired South Australian commissioner of police. His general bearing and attitude toward the Australian bush and its native inhabitants was similar to that of Major Thomas Mitchell. He regarded the bush as his enemy and the aborigines as a very low form of animal life. Like Mitchell, he seems to have been an alien in the bush landscape, which rejected him. Despite several short journeys in 1860 over part of Eyre's route along the Great Australian Bight and around Lake Torrens, he never developed the natural bushman's feeling for country. He was always at odds with his surroundings.

Warburton had great tenacity of purpose, however, and pushed on, though the country he encountered was probably the driest and most inhospitable tract ever crossed by an Australian exploration party. Blocked by sandhills and dry spinifex country, Warburton veered north of west and headed for Lake Gregory, at the termination of Sturt Creek.

Months passed and the water situation became desperate. Food supplies dwindled also. Whenever he saw aboriginal camp fires, Warburton headed for them, hoping to find large waterholes. Mostly he found only small soaks, which had to be dug out to allow his camels to drink.

At one such well, the party was marooned for six weeks until they retreated to a previous camp and struck farther north. Warburton spent a lot of time chasing aborigines, his idea being to tie them up until thirst drove them to reveal their tribal wells. A small girl he tied up escaped in the night by gnawing through her bonds.

A "howling, hideous old hag" Warburton tied up to a tree so annoyed the explorer with her wailing over several days that he finally let her go. Naturally, the aborigines gave Warburton's party a wide berth after such episodes. While they waxed fat in what was to them a land of plenty, Warburton and his men staggered on, starving and thirsty.

Three camels died. Their flesh was cut in strips and hung over the spinifex and scrub to dry in the sun. No part of the animals was wasted. The entrails were eaten first, then the head, feet and hides were cut up and boiled to make soup. The men grew weaker on this diet of camel, flour and tea. Some began to show signs of scurvy.

Near the Western Australian border, Warburton mentioned in his journal "several small Leichhardt trees", meaning a certain type of scrub, not trees marked by the explorer. This entry later gave rise to stories that signs of Leichhardt had been found in the area.

Although he knew their positions from the map of Augustus Gregory, Warburton missed Sturt Creek and Lake Gregory by a few miles. As it was a dry year, they would have offered him no comfort, in any case. At this stage, Warburton gave up any notion of making south for Perth and plodded desperately westward to the Oakover River, where he believed there were sheep stations.

He became so weak that he had to be strapped on his camel. Warburton's son also broke down and was unable to walk. Surveyor Lewis and the aborigine Charlie became the mainstays of the party as they battled west. Warburton was partially blind and his spirits low. He wrote: "My party . . . are now in that state that, unless it pleases God to save us, we cannot live more than twenty-four hours. We are at our last drop of water, and the smallest bit of dried meat chokes me . . . God have mercy upon us, for we are brought very low, and by the time death reaches us we shall not regret exchanging our present misery for the state in which the weary are at rest. We have tried to do our duty, and have been disappointed in all our expectations. The country is terrible. I do not believe men ever traversed so vast an extent of continuous desert."

In this condition, they staggered on to a tributary of the Oakover, where their water problems were solved. But they were still without food and almost too weak to move. It was December, 1873. Warburton sent Lewis and Charlie ahead with the two strongest of the three remaining camels. The nearest station proved to be almost 200 miles away, but Lewis made it and returned to save his sick and starving leader on 29th December, 1873.

Eventually the party limped to the coast and returned to Adelaide by ship. Although they had not discovered an acre of useful country, Warburton and his men had won the honour of being the first to cross from the overland telegraph line to the west coast.

Desert marathon

Giles

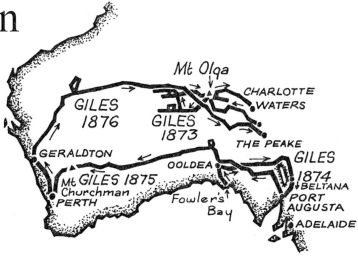

While Warburton was languishing near the Western Australian border, Ernest Giles was setting out from the overland telegraph line on his second attempt to cross to Perth. It was 4th August, 1873. Giles was accompanied by William Henry Tietkins, James Andrews and Alfred Gibson.

The last man had been recruited at the Peake Telegraph station, the expedition's starting point. Giles wrote: "He was not a man I would have picked out of a mob, but men were scarce, and as he seemed so anxious to come, and as I wanted somebody, I agreed to take him." While interviewing Gibson, Giles asked: "Can you ride? Can you starve? Can you go without water?" They were prophetic queries.

Giles was a singular man in the ranks of Australian explorers, company that was not lacking individualism. He seems to have successfully combined Leichhardt's happy confidence with Eyre's dogged stubbornness and Augustus Gregory's methodical competence. He disliked the aborigines and had little to do with them. He possessed a kind of missionary zeal which drove him on through the

toughest country and kept him cheerful in all but the direst times.

He was a selfish man, after the manner of Leichhardt, and put his ambitions ahead of the needs of other men, who had to like it or lump it. (On his first expedition, he had been prepared to send one man off into the wilderness, to find his own way back to civilization, in order to conserve rations so that he, Giles, might proceed farther. This callousness had offended the only other member of the party and caused the break-up of the expedition.)

He had a dry, sarcastic sense of humour, too. At an early camp on his second journey, a dead limb supporting a tent rope crashed on the party while they were eating. Giles wrote: "It first fell on the head of Jimmy Andrews, which broke it in half; it also fell across my back, tearing my waistcoat, shirt and skin; but as it only fell on Jimmy's head, of course it didn't hurt him."

More than any other explorer of the arid inland, Giles seemed to enjoy his work. He constantly wrote in lyrical terms of the colours, smells and sounds of the bush. Often he was unduly impressed

113

with the country, because he happened to pass through in a good season after rain. Many of his inspired names for desert places seem ludicrous today—though thunderstorms may occasionally make them briefly idyllic as Giles saw them.

As he approached Mount Olga, Giles wrote: "These grassy glades were fair to see, reminding one somewhat of Merrie England's glades and Sherwood forest's green . . ."

Describing an overnight camp in this area, he recorded: "The dew was falling fast, the night air was cool, and deliciously laden with the scented exhalations from trees and shrubs and flowers. The odour of almonds was intense, reminding me of the perfumes of the wattle blooms of the . . . more fertile portions of this continent . . ."

Thus enchanted, Giles was apt to give what are generally desolate places names such as "Fairies Glen" and "Schwerin Mural Crescent". A patch of grass or a rock pool was enough to set him quoting Shakespeare, Byron, or Adam Lindsay Gordon.

Giles named the Everard Ranges and while in sight of Mount Conner wrote: "Gibson and Jimmy . . . shot some parrots and other birds, which must have flown down the barrels of their guns, otherwise they never could have hit them, and we had an excellent supper of parrot soup."

At a river he named The Officer, Giles was threatened by a group of 150 armed aborigines. When they threw spears and taunted him, he and his men fired several shots near the warriors, which made them keep their distance.

That night there was an uneasy truce, with Giles and the aborigines camped on opposite banks of the mostly dry river-bed. There was little sleep for the explorers. ". . . the yelling of these fiends in human form, the clouds of smoke from the burning grass and bushes, and the many disagreeable odours incident to a large native village, and the yapping and howling of a lot of starving dogs, all combined to make us and our horses exceedingly restless," Giles wrote.

Several days later, the party reached Mount Olga, which Giles had sighted from the north on his previous expedition. With some disappointment, Giles noted: "Here I perceived the marks of a wagon and horses, and camel tracks; these I knew at once to be those of Gosse's expedition."

East Alligator River country, near Arnhem Land. Leichhardt passed this area in 1845. John McKinlay made a brief visit in 1865

The Negri River near the Northern Territory-Western Australia border. Alexander Forrest's optimistic report of the Kimberley area led to settlement by the Durack and MacDonald families

This eroded peak, once a tall mountain, is typical of the worn-down, decaying landscape in the Australian hinterland. Here explorers searched in vain for a "promised land"

Red, inhospitable sandhills, first encountered in western New South Wales, roll north-west across the continent to the Indian Ocean. This is the coast at Broome

114

He was pleased to find three streams of running water and went on to marvel at the great rock's singular appearance. "The appearance of this mountain is marvellous in the extreme, and baffles accurate description . . . it is formed of several vast and solid, huge and rounded blocks of bare red conglomerate stones, being composed of untold masses of rounded stones of all kinds and sizes, mixed like plums in a pudding and set in vast and rounded shapes upon the ground . . . The appearance of Mount Olga from this camp is truly wonderful; it displayed to our astonished eyes rounded minarets, giant cupolas, and monstrous domes. There they have stood as huge memorials of the ancient times of earth, for ages, countless eons of ages, since its creation first had birth. The rocks are smoothed with the attrition of the alchemy of years . . . I can only liken Mount Olga to several enormous rotund or rather elliptical shapes of rouge mange."

South-west of Mount Olga, Giles struck westward through the Mann Range, encountering good patches of storm feed and water in rock holes. At one place he came on three lowans' nests, from which he recovered a dozen eggs. He wrote: "These nests are found only in thick scrubs. I have known them five or six feet high, of a circular conical shape, and a 100 feet round the base . . ." Concerning the eggs, he remarked: ". . . they are larger than a goose egg, and of a more delicious flavour than any other egg in the world. Their shell in beautifully pink tinted, and so terribly fragile that, if a person is not careful in lifting them, the fingers will crunch through the tinted shell in an instant." Giles went on to describe how decaying vegetable matter in the mound nest supplies the warmth to incubate the eggs.

Two-storeyed aboriginal huts were discovered in this area, built of heavy boughs; also fences round waterholes which Giles assumed had been constructed to trap emus and kangaroos coming in to drink.

Farther westward, dry country was encountered and the water situation became serious. Only small, isolated rock holes could be found, some containing only a few gallons, which the horses quickly drank. At one larger pool, a group of aborigines tried to bluff the explorers away by shouting and waving their spears. Desperate, Giles moved in and sent them packing. He wrote: "No doubt (they) were dreadfully annoyed to find their little

reservoirs discovered by such water-swallowing wretches as they doubtless thought white men and horses to be: I could only console myself with the reflection, that in such a region as this we must be prepared to lay down our lives at any moment in our attempts to procure water; and we must take it when we find it at any price, life and water are synonymous terms. I dare say they know where to get more, but I don't . . . We used every drop of water."

This selfish, cavalier approach was hardly likely to win the hearts and minds of the local inhabitants, who may *not* have known where to get more water.

It was now November, 1873. The summer sun was blasting down on the landscape, turning it to red sand and dust. The explorers could find no water and retreated. One horse had to be shot. The others plodded on weakly.

Rock-holes that had sustained them on the way out were dry or putrid. Giles described one of them: "I found the hole was choked up with rotten leaves, dead animals, birds and all imaginable sorts of filth. On poking a stick down into it, seething bubbles aerated through the putrid mass, and yet the natives had evidently been living upon this fluid for some time; some of the fires in their camp were yet alight." (They didn't know of other waterholes, after all!) "I had very great difficulty in reaching down to bale any of this fluid into my canvas bucket . . ."

By shovelling large wells in the sand of creek beds, the explorers found sufficient water to keep themselves and their mounts alive. Giles and Gibson fell ill. At a large waterhole they discovered, a semi-permanent camp was established, consisting of a large bough shed the explorers named Fort Mueller, after their sponsor. Giles recovered from his illness, but Gibson's improvement was slow.

For several days, earthquakes shook the countryside, toppling huge boulders from the surrounding hills. Christmas 1873 was celebrated with a plum pudding cooked by Gibson, wallaby chops and a bottle of rum. Gibson got slightly better and the party probed due north for 120 miles. Good waterholes were found and a base camp was established. Giles called this place Sladen Water and the near-by valley that gave access to it, the Pass of the Abencerrages. This is close to the present-day Giles weather station, which is in the Rawlinson Ranges about 45 miles into Western Australia

F

from the Northern Territory border. It was now late in January, 1874.

In his journal for December and January, Giles several times quotes conversations he had with Gibson and details some of Gibson's exploits around the camp, concerning his handling of horses, his bushcraft and in particular his sense of direction. Giles also quotes remarks and opinions about Gibson expressed by his other two companions. The gist of all this is that Gibson was apparently a simple, illiterate fellow, with little common sense, even less bush sense and absolutely no sense of direction. He was forever getting lost within sight of camp, driving thirsty horses past water without giving them time to drink, and turning them out for the night without hobbles or with their packs still attached. At best, Gibson seems to have been a genial, good-natured half-wit.

This is interesting, in view of later events.

In February, the party pushed north to Mt Destruction, so named by Giles because his expedition came close to destruction when visiting the mountain. He had glimpsed it from his camp at Fort McKellar in the Rawlinsons and thought it might be the beginning of another range leading west. The Rawlinsons had petered out into desert.

The party experienced hot weather on their journey to Mt Destruction, found no water and were forced to retreat immediately to Fort Mc-Kellar. Four of their remaining 14 horses died on the return journey. Feed for the surviving horses was scarce, so Giles retreated further to his old camp at Sladen Water. Here the horses recovered some of their strength while Giles and his men feasted on wild ducks and pigeons.

Aborigines attacked the camp at Sladen Water, but were driven off by warning shots. Ants pestered the explorers at night, making sleep almost impossible.

A sortie to the south-west was foiled by sandhills and Giles once more had to retreat to his base camp. He wrote: "Oh, would that I had camels! What are horses in such a region and such a heated temperature as this."

Baffled by the dryness of the country, Giles and William Tietkins headed east toward Mt Olga. Gibson and Andrews remained at Sladen Water. Giles discovered and named the Petermann Ranges on this trip, also Gills Pinnacle, Rebecca Creek, Bloods Range and the Docker and Hull rivers (both of which were dry).

Aborigines again attacked him when he was camped at a waterhole 60 miles west of Mt Olga. Giles and Tietkins drove the warriors off with revolver shots. "Some of their spears were smashed in their hands," Giles wrote. This is an extraordinary statement and only serves to cast doubt on Giles's various accounts of brushes with aborigines.

As usual, he makes no mention of shooting any tribesmen in this affray, but if such close shooting took place, it seems probable some were wounded, if not killed. An illustration of the incident in Giles's journal shows one fallen tribesman.

Considering the number of times Giles was attacked, and the large number of tribesmen involved on each occasion, it appears unlikely they would have been repelled so effectively by a few shots over their heads and round their feet, as Giles suggests. His general remarks about aborigines indicate that he considered them no better than wild animals. In similar threatening circumstances, with their lives at stake, any explorers might have felt justified in wounding or killing their attackers in self-defence. It seems probable that Giles did just this, but he has taken pains to omit any reference to anything more than firing warning shots.

In view of this, it is possible he omitted certain facts in his account of later happenings on this journey, when a matter of life or death arose in what is now the Gibson Desert.

While the party camped at Sladen Water, rations began to run short. A horse was killed and smoked in a specially constructed smoke-house. Thunderstorms threatened several times and Giles hoped for rain to open a road west for him. He was disappointed.

Determined to make one final attempt to get farther west, Giles again shifted his base camp out to Fort McKellar. He wrote on 19th April, 1874: "I had made up my mind to try what impression 100 miles would make on the country to the west . . . When I made known my intention, Gibson immediately volunteered to accompany me, and complained of having previously been left so often and so long in the camp. I much preferred Mr. Tietkins . . . but to please Gibson, he waived his right, and, though I said nothing, I was not at all pleased."

On 20th April, Giles and Gibson set out westward. They had with them two riding horses and two pack horses. One pack animal carried a week's supply of smoked horse and two 5-gallon water kegs, plus some blankets. The other carried two 10-gallon water-bags.

Beyond the Rawlinsons they encountered sand-hills running east and west, between which they made fairly easy going. At the end of the second day, they were 60 miles out from Fort McKellar. The two pack horses were released and sent back on their tracks. Giles and Gibson gave their mounts the last of the water in the two big leather bags, after filling their own small water-bags. The two 5-gallon kegs were left hanging on a tree at this spot, which Giles called "the Kegs".

That night they pushed another 20 miles west. Next day they made another 30 miles, in fierce heat, to reach stony country with a distant low range of mountains in sight, another 30 miles away. Giles named these the Alfred and Marie ranges and turned reluctantly back on his tracks. The heat was oppressive. Men and horses faltered. After 20 miles, Gibson's horse knocked up and lay down to die.

The two men walked and rode in turns for some time, then Giles called a halt and announced he had made an extraordinary decision. Gibson was to take the horse and go ahead for 30 miles to the tree containing the two water kegs, where he was to give the horse a drink and then proceed a further 60 miles back to Fort McKellar and get help! These instructions were given to the happy duffer who had never been able to find his way to or from anywhere during the nine months the expedition had been in the field.

Giles wrote in his journal that he emphasized to Gibson that he must follow their outward tracks back to the Kegs and then to Fort McKellar. But to anyone who knows this country, such a task was clearly beyond a man like Gibson. The country is stony in parts, and only a man with an excellent sense of direction would be able to walk on to intermittent horse tracks in the sand. There are no landmarks to speak of and even a skilled bush-man would need a compass to steer a course to a single tree across 30 miles of featureless country. Gibson was a hopeless bushman.

Giles's instructions to Gibson were therefore his death warrant, if his journal report is correct.

But the explorer's description of the whole incident simply does not ring true to anyone who has been in this desert and knows something of horses.

For example, an almost knocked-up horse carry-ing a rider would plod no faster than a walking man, so where was the reason for the two men to separate? It was only 30 miles back to the Kegs, where there were 10 gallons of water waiting. After that, two men and one horse could proceed more safely together than separately, and just as fast.

Giles says he gave Gibson his Gregory's Patent compass, though he realized Gibson had no idea how to use it. Why then give it to him? Particu-larly as Giles, who had made a few errors of direc-tion earlier in the expedition, would need it himself to be sure of getting back to the Kegs. In such country, particularly under duress, the best bush-man can get "slewed" without a compass.

Whatever happened out in the desert that now bears Gibson's name, it is obvious that Giles's account of events leaves much to be desired.

However, according to Giles, he sent Gibson on his way and then proceeded himself in the same direction, on foot. He walked all day and part of the night, "until the moon went down". The Mount Stromlo Observatory reports that the moon on 24th April 1874, was just past first quarter and that taking into account its altitude of 46 degrees at Latitude 25 degrees south, the "actual illumin-ance would be rather less than 20 per cent" of the illuminance of a full moon. Giles's suggestion that he followed horse tracks by such weak illumina-tion is therefore open to grave doubt.

He reached the Kegs next day around noon, found that Gibson had been there, leaving him two gallons of water in the remaining keg. After brooding over his predicament for some time, Giles shouldered the keg and plodded eastward. Again he walked by moonlight, but next morning calculated he had gone only three miles from the Kegs. This is surprising, because on the day and night before he had travelled 30 miles. He was now burdened by a 15 pound keg containing 20 pounds of water, but only three miles in eight or 10 hours' walking is poor going indeed.

For the next three or four days, Giles wrote that he travelled only about five miles daily, in a deliri-ous, half-conscious state. He lay down and slept in the shade during the hottest hours, and travelled considerably at night. At one stage, he wrote: "I am sure I must have remained (unconscious) over 48 hours."

Amazingly, in this delirious, exhausted, almost

trance-like condition, he did not fail to note the tracks of the two released pack-horses veering off south from the outward tracks leading back to Fort McKellar. And he noted that Gibson's horse had followed these two wanderers instead of keeping to the homeward trail.

Despite his condition, Giles wrote that he followed Gibson's tracks for "about a mile and then returned to the proper line, anxiously looking at every step to see if Gibson's horse tracks returned to them. They never did".

Giles staggered into his depot camp at Fort Mc-Kellar at dawn on 1st May. It was seven days since he had left the Kegs to walk the 60-mile journey. According to his journal, he had covered less than 20 miles by the night of the 28th, so he apparently put on a tremendous spurt on the last two days to get over the remaining 40 miles. This is despite his journal entry that at this stage he could scarcely walk, was footsore and "could only go at a snail's pace".

After a day of rest, Giles and Tietkins set out on 2nd May in search of Gibson. But they rode past the point where Gibson had veered south and went first to the Kegs "to get the bags left there, and some indispensable things". It was 6th May before they got back to where Gibson had left the correct line of travel.

They followed the tracks of the three horses for a while, then saw where Gibson's mount had veered due south. This single set of tracks proved hard to follow and by noon the next day they had to give up and return to Fort McKellar. Giles wrote of his grief concerning Gibson, but concluded with a comforting line from Bunyan: "Wail not for the dead, for they have now become the companions of the immortals."

After killing and smoking another horse and re-shoeing the remainder, Giles and his party set off homeward via Mt Olga and Ayers Rock.

They met a maintenance team on the overland telegraph line on 10th July and reached Charlotte Waters three days later. The expedition had been in the field almost a year.

Giles was now convinced that he would never be able to travel overland to Perth without camels. Through his previous sponsor, Baron von Mueller, he arranged a meeting with Sir Thomas Elder who was then the only man in Australia with a sizeable camel stud. This was located at Beltana, near Lake Torrens.

Sir Thomas agreed to equip Giles for an expedition to the west, but first sent him on a journey from Fowler's Bay round the Bight to Eucla on the Western Australian border. Then Giles retraced his steps almost to Fowler's Bay and proceeded overland in a direct line through unknown country to the northern shore of Lake Torrens and round to Beltana. On this trip he used horses and camels. Before the party reached Lake Torrens, all the horses were dead. Without the camels, Giles and his men would have perished also. It was a salutory lesson for the explorer and heightened his already high regard for camels as working beasts in desert country.

The only discovery of note on this trip was an aboriginal dam, constructed on a claypan at a place known to the local tribes as Pylebuny. This is 80 miles almost due north of Fowler's Bay. The dam wall was five feet high and formed a circle, with an opening in its high side to allow water to drain in. Giles wrote: "This wall, or dam, constructed by the aboriginals, is the first piece of work of art or usefulness that I had ever seen in all my travels in Australia; and if I had only heard of it, I should seriously have reflected upon the credibility of my informant, because no attempts of skill, or ingenuity, on the part of Australian natives, applied to building, or the storage of water, have previously been met with, and I was very much astonished at beholding one now. This piece of work was two feet thick on the top of the wall, twenty yards in the length of its sweep, and at the bottom, where the water lodged, the embankment was nearly five feet thick. The clay of which this dam was composed had been dug out of the hole in which the water lay, with small native wooden shovels, and piled up to its present dimensions."

This journey was made in March and April, 1875.

On 6th May, 1875, Giles set out from Beltana, bound for Perth. He had with him an aboriginal scout, five white companions, including Tietkins as second in command, and Saleh, an Afghan camel driver. There were 15 pack camels and seven riding camels. Each of the pack camels carried a load of around 550 pounds. (A horse in similar country would not take more than 150 pounds.)

The party first went south to Port Augusta and started on the journey proper on 23rd May, 1875.

This was to be the longest-ever Australian exploring expedition, in time and distance covered. Giles was 15 months afield, mostly in desert country, over which he travelled nearly 6,000 miles!

Heading north from Port Augusta, Giles picked up his recent track near Lake Gairdner and followed it west past the aboriginal dam to his old depot camp at Youldeh, about 80 miles northwest of Fowler's Bay. (This is the present site of Ooldea, on the trans-continental railway line.) Giles visited the coast while Tietkins and a companion probed north, trying to find a route to the Musgrave Ranges. This they failed to do. Giles reconnoitred west, finding a small quantity of water in another aboriginal dam 180 miles away. He returned to Youldeh and brought the main party on.

Travel was through dense scrub and spinifex, through which the leading camels had to smash a tunnel. Giles wrote: ". . . (the spinifex) took every hair off their legs up to three feet from the ground, and their limbs turned black, and were as bright and shiny as a newly-polished boot."

While scouting south for water, he came into the clear country of the Nullarbor Plain and noted in his journal: "It was splendid country for the camels to travel over; no spinifex, no impediments for their feet, and no timber. A bicycle could be ridden, I believe, over the whole extent of this plain, which must be 500 or 600 miles long by nearly 200 miles broad."

Rain fell, so that when the dam was reached, Giles found it overflowing, with a depth of six feet of water in it. This dam was located just inside the Western Australian border, among what are now called the Forrest Lakes in the Great Victoria Desert. The party camped for a week while the camels regained condition on the rich herbage.

But the water supply was rapidly drying up and Giles was in a quandary, which is best explained by him: "It appeared evident to me, as I had traversed nothing but scrubs for hundreds of miles from the east, and had found no water of any size whatever . . . that no waters really existed in this country, except an occasional native well or dam, and those only at considerable distances apart. Concluding this to be the case, and my object being that the expedition should reach the city of Perth, I decided . . . to go thither, at any risk, and trust to Providence for an occasional supply of water here and there . . . I desired to make for a

hill or mountain called Mount Churchman by Augustus Churchman Gregory in 1846. I had no written record of water existing there, but my chart showed that Mount Churchman had been visited by two or three other travellers since that date, and it was presumable that water did permanently exist there.

"The hill was, however, distant from this dam considerably over 600 miles in a straight line, and too far away for it to be possible we could reach it unless we should discover some new watering places between . . . Where the next favoured spot would be found, who could tell?

". . . Having considered all these matters, I informed my officers and men that I had determined to push westward, without a thought of retreat, no matter what the result might be; that it was a matter of life or death for us; we must push through or die in the scrubs. I added that if any more than one of the party desired to retreat, I would provide them with rations and camels, when they could either return to Fowler's Bay . . . or descend to Eucla station on the coast, which lay south nearly 170 miles distant.

"I represented that we were probably in the worst desert upon the face of the earth, but that fact would give us all the more pleasure in conquering it . . . It was of course a desperate thing to do and I believe few people would or could rush madly into a totally unknown wilderness, where the nearest known water was 650 miles away. But I had sworn to go to Perth or die in the attempt, and I inspired the whole of my party with my own enthusiasm. One and all declared they would live or die with me."

The party set off westward on 10th September, 1875. In 10 days they travelled almost 200 miles. Apart from one brief shower of rain, they saw no water. There were "some murmurs of regret" among the men, particularly from Saleh, the Afghan camel driver. Giles recorded: "Whenever we camped, Saleh would stand before me, gaze fixedly into my face and generally say: 'Mister Gile, when you get water?' I pretended to laugh at the idea, and say: 'Water? pooh! there's no water in this country, Saleh. I didn't come here to find water, I came here to die, and you said you'd come and die too.' Then he would ponder awhile, and say: 'I think some camel he die to-morrow, Mr. Gile.' I would say: 'No, Saleh, they can't possibly live till to-morrow, I think they will die tonight.' Then he: 'Oh, Mr. Gile, I think we all die soon now.' Then I: 'Oh, yes, Saleh, we'll all be dead in a day or two.' When he found he couldn't get any satisfaction out of me he would begin to pray, and ask me which was the east. I would point south: down he would go on his knees, and abase himself in the sand, keeping his head in it for some time. Afterwards he would have a smoke, and I would ask: 'What's the matter, Saleh? what have you been doing?' 'Ah, Mr. Gile,' was his answer, 'I pray to my God to give you a rock-hole tomorrow.' I said, 'Why, Saleh, if the rock-hole isn't there already there won't be time for your God to make it; besides, if you can get what you want by praying for it, let me have a fresh-water lake, or a running river, that will take us right away to Perth. What's the use of a paltry rock-hole?' Then he said solemnly, 'Ah, Mr. Gile, you not religious.' "

On the thirteenth day, the 18 camels were given their first drink from the water barrels they carried: four gallons each, which, Giles remarked "was about equivalent to four thimblesful to a man".

On the sixteenth day, Giles estimated his party was 500 miles from the Youldeh depot. Late in the afternoon, he noticed that Jess Young, his third officer, was leading the camel string slightly off the expedition's chosen course. Giles corrected him and was told curtly: "Perhaps you'll steer, then, if you don't think I can!"

Luckily Giles did. Next day the party came unexpectedly on a miraculous oasis Giles named Queen Victoria's Spring. Had they continued on the incorrect course of the previous day, they would have missed it by several miles. As it was, Giles gave the credit for finding the water jointly to his second in command, Tietkins, and Tommy, the aboriginal scout.

Tietkins had a premonition that water was near and sent Tommy to scout for animal tracks that might lead to it. The expedition was in featureless sand-hill country and was passing almost one mile north of the spring when Tommy rejoined the string, shouting hysterically: "Water! Water! Plenty water here! Come on! Come on! This way! This way! Come on, Mr. Giles! Mine been find 'em plenty water!"

The party stayed at Queen Victoria's Spring for nine days, then set out once more for Perth, on 6th October, 1875. On the 13th, after travelling 200 miles, the explorers found another spring,

where they met the first aborigines they had encountered on their journey. The place was called Ularring.

The aborigines seemed very friendly. Several of them, including a small, cheerful imp of a girl, spent most of their time in Giles's camp. One man wore a pearl-shell ornament round his neck. (Ularring is 300 miles from the sea.) But on 16th October, just after they had finished their evening meal, Giles and his men were attacked by a war party of 100 warriers. As they grabbed up their guns, the "friendly" aborigines in the camp attacked them with tomahawks.

Giles wrote: "This was the best organized and most disciplined aboriginal force I ever saw." Strangely, none of the explorers was injured, and soon "the routed army, carrying their wounded, disappeared behind the trees . . ."

Giles left Ularring on 18th October, 1875. They crashed and tore their way through dense scrub for more than 150 miles, to reach Mount Churchman on 27th October. Giles described it as "a small hill" but was pleased to find a native well with plenty of water.

On 4th November, the explorers reached an outlying sheep station, where they were welcomed by an astonished Irish shepherd, thus: "Holy sailor, what's that? Is it South Australia yez come from? Shure I cam from there meself. Did yez crass any say? I don't know, sure I came by Albany; I never came the way you've come at all. Shure, I wilcome yez, in the name of the whole colony. I saw something about yez in the paper not long ago. Can I do anything for yez?"

The journey through the settled districts to Perth was a triumphal progress for the explorers. They were feted along the way, attending public dinners and banquets almost daily. Eager crowds lined the streets of Fremantle and Perth, but poor Giles had trouble with his riding camel and had to dismount and lead her "so that I was hidden in the crowd, and Mr. Tietkins, coming next to me, appeared to be the leader, as his camel went all right. The balconies and verandahs here were also thronged with ladies, who showered down heaps of garlands while they cheered. I was completely hidden, and they threw all the flowers down on Tietkins, so that he got all the honour from the ladies . . ."

Such are the cruel disappointments that beset the Australian explorer, even in his triumph.

Champagne flowed freely for several days, in which the explorers washed away the dust of 2,500 miles on the track. Giles wrote: "The wine merchants became nervous lest the supply of what then became known as 'Elder wine' should get exhausted." (Sir Thomas Elder had financed the expedition.)

But Giles did not linger too long in Perth. On 13th January, 1876, he was at the head of his camel string again, heading north for Geraldton. From there he intended to set a north-west course to the same degree of latitude he had been following west with the ill-fated Gibson. He would then head due east for the Alfred and Marie Range he had glimpsed on the day he and Gibson began their retreat to Fort McKellar.

Tietkins had gone home to Adelaide by ship, saying he had private business to attend to. So had Giles's third in command, Jess Young, with whom he had clashed several times on the journey. Giles wrote that he was sorry to lose Tietkins, but "I did not request Mr. Young to accompany me on my return journey".

His companions on this trip were Alec Ross, promoted to second in command, Peter Nicholls, cook on the outward trip, Saleh the Afghan camel driver and the aboriginal scout, Tommy Oldham.

The party met with champagne and free lunches all the way to Geraldton, where they arrived on 16th February, 1876. It was good drinking weather—the temperature was frequently 115 degrees Fahrenheit.

A few days out of Geraldton, at Cheangwa, the last station on the Murchison River, several comely aboriginal girls offered to come with the explorers. Giles recorded: "One interesting young person in undress uniform came up to me and said 'This is Judy, I am Judy. You Melbourne walk? Me Melbourne walk too.' I said 'Oh, all right, my dear'; to this she replied, 'Then you'll have to gib me dress.' I gave her a shirt."

On 8th April, Giles was still camped at Pia Spring. Eventually he set out on 10th April, bound for Mount Hale, on the upper Murchison River.

By May, Giles and his men were slogging through inhospitable country which he described as "stony, sterile, and hideous, and totally unsuited for the occupation or habitation of the white man". This was near the headwaters of the Ashburton River, about 75 miles south of the present mining town of Newman. The party discovered good water in a picturesque spot Giles named Glen Ross, after his second in command, Alec Ross. Giles at this point was having serious eye trouble and therefore named a line of hills that blocked his northern progress the Ophthalmia Range.

The heat was intense and myriads of flies tortured the travellers. Giles was completely blind and had to be led about by Ross. The expedition established a base camp on good water at a junction of the Ashburton and one of its tributaries near what is now Bulloo Downs station.

The weather cooled and Giles's eye condition improved during the last days of May. On 1st June, 1876, the party set off eastward into the Gibson Desert. Giles wrote: "The question which now arose was, what kind of country existed between us and my farthest watered point in 1874 at the Rawlinson Range? In a perfectly straight line it would be 450 miles."

Giles soon found out. There was no water and a bush poisonous to camels was common. He spent much of his time nursing the sick animals.

By digging a well 15 feet deep, the explorers gained enough water to push on. Grass trees (Xanthorrhoea), more common in well-watered country, grew on the sand ridges. The camels became weak.

At an abandoned aboriginal camp, Giles found a soak that required only three feet of digging to produce water. At 230 miles from the deep well they had dug, the explorers reached "a little trifling water-channel, with a few small scattered white gum-trees", where they dug a shallow tank to water the camels. One old cow, named Buzoe, collapsed and died at this camp, which Giles called Buzoe's Grave.

Pushing on, Giles wrote of the countryside: "It rolled along in ceaseless undulations of sand. The only vegetation besides the ever-abounding spinifex was a few blood-wood trees . . . with an occasional desert oak, an odd patch or clump of mallee-trees, standing desolately alone, and perhaps having a stunted specimen or two of the quandong or native peach-tree growing among them. The region is so desolate that it is horrifying even to describe."

Giles at last reached the Alfred and Marie Range, but found the hills so insignificant, he quickly passed them by. On 1st July, 1876, "the well-remembered features of the Rawlinson Range and the terrible Mount Destruction rose at last upon my view. On reaching the range, I suppose I may say that the exploring part of my expedition was at an end, for I had twice traversed Australia", Giles wrote.

The explorer now followed his old tracks to Mt Olga, Ayers Rock and the overland telegraph line, reaching the Peake Telegraph station on 23rd August, 1876.

After resting there a few days, Giles and his men continued south to Beltana, where the camels were returned to their depot. The explorers then took a coach to the Burra Burra copper mines, 100 miles north of Adelaide. There a banquet was held in their honour. Next day they boarded a southbound train. At Gawler the train was delayed while some local dignitaries made speeches and champagne flowed. In Adelaide, crowds were waiting and at a reception in the Town Hall, the "Elder wine" again flowed copiously.

But Giles's hour of glory seems to have been brief, and his rewards small, despite his monumental, unprecedented achievements. He had, after all, discovered nothing useful.

He noted, on the last page of his journal: "The time I expended (on exploration) was five of the best years of my life. As a recognition of my labours, I have received the Patron's Gold Medal of the Royal Geographical Society of London; and the late King Victor Emanuel sent me a decoration and diploma of Knighthood, of the Order of the Crown of Italy."

Such are the rewards of desert wayfarers.

The vast tract of semi-desert country enclosed by Ernest Giles's various journeys, totalling more than half a million square miles, is little changed from the 1870s. In places where grazing has been introduced, or rabbits have flourished, it is even more desolate and inhospitable.

This is spinifex, sand and mulga country, with a high proportion of stony land, still difficult to traverse even in modern four-wheel drive vehicles. Waterholes are rare and unreliable. Australia's last nomadic aborigines, the Pintubis, wandered here until the middle 1960s.

The transcontinental railway crosses the Nullarbor Plain well south of Giles's westward journey of 1875. To this day there is no road. From Wiluna in Western Australia to Ayers Rock in the Northern Territory, a rough four-wheel drive track known as "the Gunbarrel Highway" approximately follows Giles's 1876 eastward route. (The Forrest brothers crossed in 1874 via a parallel course, farther south, through country where there is still no semblance of a track.) A reasonable good weather road now connects the settlement of Laverton with the Warburton aboriginal mission near the Blackstone Range.

Apart from a few temporary graded tracks constructed by government surveyors and geologists, the Great Victoria and Gibson deserts remain almost completely inaccessible. Aboriginal reserves now enclose much of the country first seen by Giles and his companions.

John Forrest's 1874 expedition, from Geraldton on the west coast to the Overland Telegraph line, under attack from aborigines at Weld Springs

Overleaf: Geike Gorge, on the southern border of the Kimberleys. George Grey first approached this region from the coast in 1837. Alexander Forrest made further explorations in 1879

Colonel Warburton shelters in a sandstorm over the Great Sandy Desert on his 1873 expedition

125

Near Lake Carnegie in Western Australia, on the edge of the country explored by John Forrest (1874) and Ernest Giles (1876)

The Gunbarrel "highway" across the Gibson Desert, a rough 4-wheel drive track, hard to find in places in dry, dust-storm weather. No petrol or supplies can be bought between Wiluna and Curtin Springs, a track journey of about 1,100 miles

Some lesser-known explorers

Lindsay and others

We have followed the adventures of the best known figures of Australian exploration, but there were scores of other men who risked their lives to blaze new trails to a hoped-for Promised Land. Many of them led small privately-financed parties in search of new grazing lands for their backers. Men in this category were sheep and cattlemen such as Patrick Leslie, Nat Buchanan, the Mac-Donalds and the Duracks, Alfred Giles, Patrick Drinan, the Prout brothers, Carr Boyd, John Duke Graham, Duncan Macgregor and Sylvester Browne.

Among the lesser known explorers who led organized expeditions into the interior were these men: David Lindsay, who took a government expedition to Arnhem Land in 1883, finishing at Katherine, five months later. In 1885, Lindsay crossed the lower Simpson Desert from the Finke River to the Queensland border. Returning to the Finke, he skirted the western edge of the desert, then travelled north-east to Lake Nash, near the present Queensland border, completing his journey at the mouth of the Macarthur River on the Gulf of Carpentaria. In 1891 he led an expedition for Sir Thomas Elder from the Rawlinson Range south-west to Queen Victoria Springs, then north-west to the Murchison River. He reported gold-bearing country around Coolgardie and Kalgoorlie.

In 1894, explorer C. Winnecke led the A. W. Horn scientific expedition into central Australia. He was accompanied by Baldwin Spencer and Frank Gillen, who later made a number of journeys in the centre country and far north between 1900 and 1913. (Winnecke had explored the Jervois Ranges and the northern edge of the Simpson Desert in 1878-81.)

Lawrence Wells, a surveyor on the Queensland-Northern Territory border during 1883-6, accompanied Lindsay on some of his journeys. In 1896, he led a disastrous expedition from the Meekatharra district in Western Australia to the Fitzroy River. Several men died. The southern portion of the Canning "stock route" roughly parallels Lawrence Wells's route.

David Wynford Carnegie led a prospecting expedition from Coolgardie to Hall's Creek and back in 1896. Lake Carnegie today bears his name. The party travelled 3,000 miles across desert country, finding water by tying up aborigines and feeding them saltbeef until they revealed their hidden wells. One such spring was hidden 25 feet underground in a cave with a tiny entrance. Called Empress Spring, it was rediscovered in 1966 by J. Rowlands while on an expedition for the Institute of Aboriginal Studies. It is located 40 miles north of the Laverton-Warburton mission road near a rocky tableland called Breaden Bluff.

Other minor Australian explorers included Barclay (1878), Mason (1896), Hubbe (1896), Hann (1896-8), Russell (1897), Rudall (1897), Maurice and Murray (1901-2).

Edmund Colson became the first man to cross

the Simpson Desert, in 1936. He started from his property on the western fringe of the desert with an aboriginal companion and several camels, reaching Birdsville 16 days later. After a brief rest, he returned over the same route.

Rhodes Scholar Dr Cecil Thomas Madigan, who had flown over the Simpson Desert in 1929, crossed it with camels in 1939. He set out from Charlotte Waters with seven men and 19 camels, charting over 1,000 sand ridges in the 300-mile journey to Birdsville.

Michael Terry the prospector was among the first motorized explorers of the far inland. He made a number of pioneering car journeys across the north of Australia and to the Centre in the 1920s and 30s. He travelled extensively with camels in the same period.

All the men of this chapter were trail-blazers of varying importance, but it can be said that the golden age of Australian exploration had ended by 1880. The last major discovery of useful new country was made by Alexander Forrest in the Kimberleys in 1879.

The giants of Australian exploration were, in chronological order: Ensign Francis Barrallier, Hamilton Hume, Captain Charles Sturt, Surveyor Augustus Churchman Gregory, John McKinlay, John McDouall Stuart, John Forrest and Ernest Giles. Judging from their journals, Barrallier seems to have been the most likeable man, Hume the most confident, Gregory the most competent, Giles the most determined, McKinlay and Forrest the luckiest, Sturt and Stuart the unluckiest.

It is difficult to judge who was the greatest explorer of them all.

Equipment for re-exploration

I took facsimile copies of all the original journals and maps of exploration I could locate, being more than a score of volumes and some 40 maps. Also, I used oil company and motorists' association maps of the more settled areas and military survey maps of the remoter regions. At all times, when travelling in lonely places, I sought local advice from settlers and aborigines, just as the early explorers did.

Keeping in mind that the most successful early expeditions were those which travelled light, I carried a minimum of equipment and supplies. Everything went comfortably into my single vehicle: a long wheelbase Land Rover (my journeys between 1954-67 were in a 4-cylinder model; after that I changed to the 6-cylinder model).

MY BASIC EQUIPMENT AND RATIONS

1 Sponge-rubber mattress
1 Hotham sleeping bag
1 Silva 15TD prismatic-type compass
1 Douglas protractor
1 Spindler SR5 transceiver
3 billies, 1 Bedourie oven, 1 quart-pot
Assorted cutlery, tin plates, plastic mixing and wash-up bowls
1 wire shelf for grilling on campfire
Lightweight 6 x 8 japara tent, additionally waterproofed at home by painting with mixture of hot kerosene and 2 lb. of dissolved paraffin wax
1 long-handled spade
1 light axe
1 bushman's saw

1 medium soft suitcase of suitably sturdy, easily washed clothing, including synthetic non-iron shirts and shorts
1 oilskin jacket, with hood
1 month's supply of food, largely tinned and dried
Up to 20 gallons of water, in 2 and 5 gallon plastic cans
Up to 74 gallons of petrol, in 14 4½ gallon jerrycans, plus the main tank, giving a range of 1,258 miles
2 spare wheels, with fittings to allow them to be used as duals on the rear wheels when required
Assorted vehicle spare parts, including all standard spares such as distributor points and cap, spark plugs, radiator hoses, plus wheel bearings, gravity petrol tank in case of fuel pump failure, tow rope, exhaust outlet heightener, etc.
Range of tools, plus a workshop manual and spare parts manual
1 puncture repair outfit and spark-plug pump
Engine oil for complete change, plus topping up
Transmission and differential oils, with pump
Notebooks
1 tape recorder and six 90 minute tapes
Spare batteries for motor drive, recorder and torch
Torch and dashboard trouble light

Camera equipment:
2 Nikon F reflex cameras with the following lenses—28mm, 50mm, 105mm, 135mm, 200mm and 200-600mm zoom
1 electric motor drive

1 large Miller tripod with senior D head
Filters, close-up attachments and small accessories
1 Gossen Sixtar exposure meter
1 Weston IV exposure meter
Up to 100 rolls of 35mm Pan F film (36 exp. cassettes)
Up to 50 rolls of 35mm Kodachrome 11 film (20 exp.)
Up to 20 rolls of 35mm Ektachrome X film (20 exp.)

Compare my list of supplies with the list from the journal of Hume and Hovell:

7 pack saddles
1 riding saddle
8 stands of arms
6 pounds of gunpowder
60 rounds of ball cartridge
6 suits of slops
6 blankets for the men
2 tarpaulins
1 tent made of coarse Colonial woollen cloth
1,200 pounds of flour
350 pounds of pork
175 pounds of sugar
38 pounds of tea and coffee
8 pounds of tobacco for the men
16 pounds of soap
20 pounds of salt
cooking utensils
1 false horizon
1 sextant
3 pocket compasses
1 perambulator (a wheeled device for recording distance travelled)
Messrs. Hovell and Hume's own personal clothes and bedding, the latter consisting, like that of the men, of a blanket only

My method of transport was fast, luxurious and comparatively safer than that of the explorers. Unlike them, I always knew what lay ahead and to either side of me. In the event of a breakdown or accident, there was the comforting presence of the transceiver, which had a range of several hundred miles. It was used also for sending and receiving telegrams, via the Australia-wide Royal Flying Doctor radio network, so I rarely experienced the loneliness of absolute isolation that gnawed at many early travellers.

My course was rarely more than a handful of miles from the original routes of exploration. I can fairly say that for the most part I have been mostly within a stone's throw of the tracks they followed and that I have seen all that can be seen today of what they saw.

The country is no longer the same, except in a handful of isolated areas. Over most of the continent, man and his livestock have wrought a change. In what used to be virgin country there are now farms and fences. Lonely camp sites are today cities and towns. Dense bushland has become open paddocks. Narrow tracks are wide bitumen highways. Industrial chimneys belch into skies that once saw only the occasional smoke of native fires. Old, reliable inland waterholes are choked with the harvest of erosion: sand. Flats between ridges where good grazing could be found after rain are bare claypans now. Once common species of bushes and trees are almost vanished, eaten down by stock or ringbarked by rabbits and goats. Artesian bores flow wastefully in places where water was once considered the most precious commodity in the world. The aborigine the explorers knew, at home in his own land, is all but vanished from the scene.

Ernest Giles at the Glen of Palms, now known as Palm Valley

Reading

Explorers' (published) journals:

Bennett, G.—WANDERINGS IN NEW SOUTH WALES (2 volumes)

Bland, W.—JOURNEY TO PORT PHILLIP

Bride, T. F.—EDITED LETTERS FROM VICTORIAN PIONEERS

Carnegie, David—SPINIFEX AND SAND

Carron, William—NARRATIVE OF AN EXPEDITION

Eyre, Edward John—JOURNALS OF EXPEDITIONS INTO CENTRAL AUSTRALIA (2 volumes)

Field, B.—GEOGRAPHICAL MEMOIRS OF NEW SOUTH WALES

Forrest, Alexander—EXPLORATION OF WEST AUSTRALIA

Forrest, John—EXPLORATION IN AUSTRALIA

Forrest, John—JOURNAL OF WESTERN AUSTRALIAN EXPLORING EXPEDITION

Giles, Ernest—AUSTRALIA TWICE TRAVERSED (2 volumes)

Gosse, William Christie—EXPLORATIONS IN CENTRAL AUSTRALIA

Gregory, Augustus and Frank—JOURNALS OF AUSTRALIAN EXPLORATION

Grey, George—TWO EXPEDITIONS OF DISCOVERY (2 volumes)

Hawdon, Joseph—JOURNAL OF A JOURNEY FROM NEW SOUTH WALES TO ADELAIDE

Hovell, William—AN ANSWER TO A BRIEF STATEMENT OF FACT

Hume, Hamilton—A BRIEF STATEMENT OF FACT

Landsborough, William—JOURNAL OF EXPEDITION

Leichhardt, Ludwig—JOURNAL OF AN OVERLAND EXPEDITION IN AUSTRALIA

Lhotsky, John—JOURNEY FROM SYDNEY TO THE AUSTRALIAN ALPS

Mackaness, George (editor)—FOURTEEN JOURNEYS OVER THE BLUE MOUNTAINS

McKinlay, John—JOURNAL OF EXPLORATION

Madigan, C. T.—ACROSS THE DEAD HEART

Mann, John Frederic—EIGHT MONTHS WITH DR. LEICHHARDT

Oxley, John—TWO EXPEDITIONS INTO NEW SOUTH WALES

Phillip, Arthur—EXTRACTS OF LETTERS

Spencer, Baldwin—WANDERING IN WILD AUSTRALIA

Stokes, Captain J. Lort—DISCOVERIES IN AUSTRALIA

Strzelecki, Paul Edmund—REPORT OF AN EXPEDITION OF EXPLORATION

Stuart, John McDouall—EXPLORATIONS

Sturt, Charles—EXPEDITIONS INTO CENTRAL AUSTRALIA (2 volumes)

Tench, William—A COMPLETE ACCOUNT OF THE SETTLEMENT OF NEW SOUTH WALES

Terry, Michael—ACROSS UNKNOWN AUSTRALIA

Tietkins, W.—NULLARBOR PLAINS

Warburton, Peter Egerton—JOURNEY ACROSS THE WESTERN INTERIOR OF AUSTRALIA

Waugh, D. L.—3 YEARS' PRACTICAL EXPERIENCE AS A SETTLER

Winnecke, C.—JOURNAL OF THE HORN SCIENTIFIC EXPEDITION TO CENTRAL AUSTRALIA

Newspapers and periodicals:

Historical Records of New South Wales

Royal Australian Historical Society Journals

Royal Geographical Society of London Proceedings

THE EMPIRE newspaper

THE ILLUSTRATED SYDNEY NEWS newspaper

THE TOWN AND COUNTRY JOURNAL

THE SYDNEY MORNING HERALD

Other books of reference:

Barker, H. M.—CAMELS AND THE OUTBACK

Barker, H. M.—DROVING DAYS

Chisholm, Alec—STRANGE NEW LAND

Cumpston, J. H. L.—THE INLAND SEA AND THE GREAT RIVER

Durack, Mary—KINGS IN GRASS CASTLES

Favenc, Ernest—THE EXPLORATION OF AUSTRALIA

Grimm, G.—THE AUSTRALIAN EXPLORERS

Joy, William—THE EXPLORERS

King, C. J.—AN OUTLINE OF CLOSER SETTLEMENT IN NEW SOUTH WALES

Morphett, George—JOHN AINSWORTH HORROCKS

Palmer, Helen (with Jessie MacLeod)—THE FIRST 100 YEARS

Scott, G. F.—THE ROMANCE OF AUSTRALIAN EXPLORATION

Shaw, A. G. L.—THE ECONOMIC DEVELOPMENT OF AUSTRALIA

Smith, Eleanor—THE BECKONING WEST

Ward, Russel—THE AUSTRALIAN LEGEND

Index

136

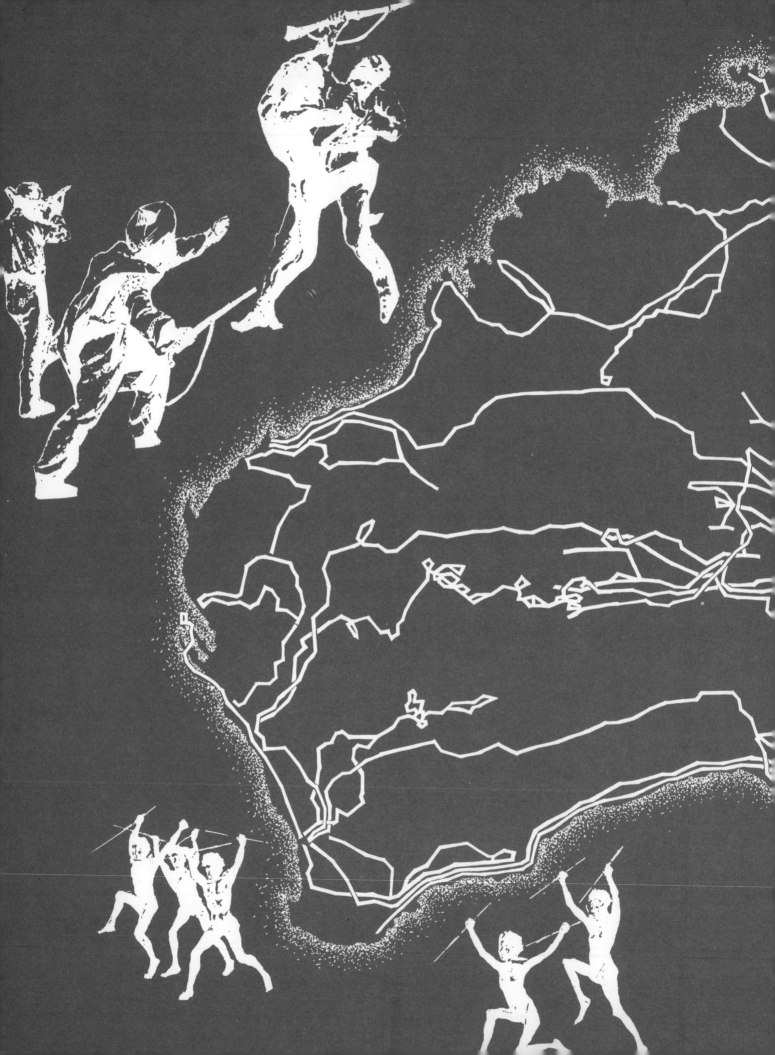